Rotisserie Grilling Cookbook

ROTISSERIE

GRILLING COOKBOOK

Easy Recipes and Step-by-Step Instructions for Mastering the Grill

JARED PULLMAN

ROCKRIDGE PRESS

Paperback ISBN: 978-1-63878-432-6
eBook ISBN: 978-1-68539-393-9

Manufactured in the United States of America

Interior and Cover Designer: Darren Samuel
Art Producer: Samantha Ulban
Editor: Anne Lowrey
Production Editor: Matthew Burnett
Production Manager: Holly Haydash

Photography © Shutterstock, Cover; © Darren Muir, pp. ii, vi; 38, 78, StockFood / Gräfe & Unzer Verlag / Schardt, Wolfgang, p. x; © Antonis Achilleos, p. 24; StockFood / PhotoCuisine, p. 26; Marija Vidal, pp. 62; 98; 108.
Author photograph courtesy of Michelle Witbeck.

10 9 8 7 6 5 4 3 2 1

This book is dedicated to everyone who told me my barbecue was good, long before it actually was.

CONTENTS

INTRODUCTION

Cooking over fire is something that takes time, patience, and dedication. I am so excited to share my favorite recipes with you, so you can delight and impress your family and friends, and also to offer tips and tricks that will dramatically improve your results. My hope is that you will no longer spend precious time and money on underwhelming rotisserie meals.

Learning to cook over fire has been a journey for me. Growing up in New Zealand, I learned about hangi, a traditional style of Maori cooking, which involves building a huge fire to heat up volcanic rocks that are placed in a hole in the ground. The food is stacked on top and covered with leaves or hessian sacks and then with dirt. The food is cooked low and slow until it's juicy, smoky, and tender.

At 20, when I moved to Australia, I engaged with a growing barbecue scene focused on low and slow cooking. But it was when I moved to the United States that my understanding of this type of cooking really took off. Low and slow refers to cooking at low temperatures over a long period of time. The United States barbecue tradition inspired me to begin cooking barbecue at least once or twice a week.

Making good barbecue (which is a technique, not a piece of equipment) comes from making bad barbecue. As I was developing my skills on the rotisserie, I researched everything I could find, from cookbooks to YouTube. This was helpful but, ultimately, there is no substitute for experience. So, I started experimenting. Over time, through trial, error, and overcooked meat, incorporating the things I had learned from watching the preparation of hangi and American style barbecue, I learned how to make great barbecue. I even began to share my insights with thousands of people on my Instagram @_howlowcanyouslow.

I just love barbecue in all of its forms. But because books can't be the size of a grill, I chose to share just one highly delicious subset of barbecue with you here, rotisserie cooking. It is flexible; it can be done on charcoal, gas, or pellets. Most cookers have a rotisserie attachment available or built-in. You don't need to spend a lot of money. This book is designed to use whatever style and type of rotisserie you have. Cooking rotisserie is easy to learn, as it almost cooks itself. You just need this book and a little bit of practice.

This book is broken into two sections. The first section is about how to master your rotisserie and outlines the techniques, tricks, and skills needed to get the most out of the 45 recipes in the book. The second section contains the recipes. Technically, these recipes could be cooked in the oven but will do best on the rotisserie in a gas or charcoal cooker. Each chapter is broken into a single topic or protein and contains recipes from cuisines and barbecue styles from around the world. Start envisioning warm Embered Potatoes (page 30) next to a slice of tender Mustard and Apricot Ham (page 66).

So, whether you want to be the house on the block that always has those amazing, smoky smells emanating from it, or if you just never want to have to order a pizza *after* slaving over the grill all day, this book is for you. Let's get into it and start making epic barbecue on the rotisserie.

Spit-Roasted Pineapple **31**

CHAPTER 1

MASTERING YOUR ROTISSERIE GRILL

Making amazing low and slow cooked food is about far more than great recipes. It results from an understanding of how smoke, fire, spices, and meat interact to produce unforgettable meals.

This chapter covers the techniques you need to produce mouthwatering barbecue every single time.

Why Rotisserie?

Growing up in New Zealand, backyard barbecues consisted of burnt hot dogs and burgers with sliced white bread instead of hamburger buns. For me, this was barbecue, the height of outdoor cuisine.

And then, everything changed. I was invited to attend a party at a friend's house. When I was still nearly a block away, I was greeted by the greatest aroma I had ever encountered. As I turned into the driveway, I found the source. A full pig, slowly turning above a charcoal fire. This was the first time I had encountered true low (temperature) and slow (timing) rotisserie cooking, and I was instantly hooked.

Rotisserie cooking has been around for, literally, thousands of years. In medieval cuisine, rotisserie cooking was the preferred method to cook large joints of meat. It is defined by meat and food being skewered on a long rod that slowly rotates over the fire as it cooks. The slow rotation helps keep the meat from burning and allows the juices and fats to slowly self-baste the exterior of the meat. This basting creates tender, juicy, incredibly flavorful food, which can be hard to achieve with other cooking methods. The bonus is that rotisserie cooking is probably one of the easiest ways to learn to barbecue low and slow.

If that isn't enough to entice you, rotisserie cooking is a true community experience. Some of the best memories I have involve sitting around a fire, turning a joint of meat with friends and family. The smell of roasting meat is in the air, people are laughing and telling stories, and everyone is anticipating the meal to come.

When was the last time you saw that happen around a pile of burnt hot dogs?

Rotisserie Grilling 101

Cooking meat low and slow is all about building layers of flavor and combining techniques to produce something unique. It is by understanding and using these various techniques and tips that you are able to produce the kind of barbecue on the rotisserie that most people only dream about making. This section explores these components—ingredients, trussing, spinning, spitting, and time and temperature—and how you can manipulate them to produce dazzling results.

Ingredients: People have been barbecuing in various incarnations all over the world for hundreds, even thousands, of years. Commonly, they all used local ingredients and seasonings to flavor their food. These flavors and ingredients vary but often include salt, sugar, herbs, spices, and produce to bring unique and powerful flavors to foods.

The best barbecue has seasoning layered throughout preparation and cooking. For instance, you might start with a brine to tenderize and begin to flavor the meat. Next, you could add a dry rub to bring punchy flavors to the dish. And, finally, you can apply a sauce throughout the cooking process to add more flavor complexity. When done correctly, good seasoning should bring something to all (or most!) of the senses and enhance the food's natural flavor.

Trussing, Spinning, and Spitting: These techniques are intended to get the most consistent and even results while cooking. I detail this subject in Trussing and Spitting Like a Pro (see page 9).

Time and Temperature: There is a saying in rotisserie barbecue: It's ready when it's ready. Because every piece of meat and every cooker is unique, it can be hard to give an accurate cooking time. So, the cook times given for the recipes in this book are an approximation to help you plan your meal. Much more important than time are: a) the doneness temperature; and b) the doneness indicators (like color and texture). When the meat hits the right internal temperature (a number I include for each recipe), it is ready to remove from the heat.

The ambient temperature in the cooker is also important; this measure describes how hot you want your cooker to be while your meat cooks. I'll go into more detail on how to control and manage this (see Preparing to Grill, page 14) in a bit.

Another aspect of getting the temperature right is positioning your food correctly in relationship to the heat source. Cooking over direct heat, as the term implies, involves placing the food directly above the heat source. This is ideal for hot and fast cooks, like searing a steak. If you were to attempt to cook something large, like a pork shoulder, directly over the flames, however, you would end up with a burnt exterior and a raw middle.

This is where indirect cooking comes in. Cooking over indirect heat means that you place the rotisserie rod near enough to the heat source to expose the food to the heat, but not directly above the flames. This technique utilizes the ambient temperature within your cooker to cook your food low and slow.

Safety First

When cooking over fire, it is important to have a good understanding of your cooker and how to handle it safely. Eye patches may look cool on pirates, but they probably won't fit your aesthetic.

Check the weather: Avoid cooking in high winds or when the danger of fire is high.

Drip pans: Drip pans help keep fats and oils away from the fire. They also make cleanup a breeze. They are the Swiss army knife of rotisserie cooking.

Grill mitts: You will likely have to pick up hot food and move burning coals while rotisserie cooking. Unless you want an impromptu visit to the emergency room, invest in a pair of sturdy, heat-resistant gloves.

Internal temperature: When cooking big joints of meat, it can be hard to know if your food is cooked thoroughly and safely. Always check the temperature with a meat thermometer, or your party may be memorable for all the wrong reasons. I recommend using a wireless thermometer like Meater. Meater measures both the internal temperature of the meat and the ambient temperature inside the cooker. It also connects directly with your phone through its app. Consistently clean your thermometer and equipment to avoid cross contamination.

Location, location, location: Always set up your cooker on a sturdy, level surface, away from branches, ceilings, walls, and neighbors who think you won't notice missing steaks.

Starter fuel: Sometimes charcoal can appear to have gone out. Do not add lighter fluid to ignite it again. Instead, keep your eyebrows by using a charcoal chimney and some tumbleweed igniters (natural wood fire starters).

User manual: Before cooking with your rotisserie, make sure you understand the safety features of your cooker.

Weight limits/weight distribution: Rotisserie cooking involves the food slowly rotating while it cooks. If your food is too heavy or unbalanced on the rotisserie, you may ruin your food or even damage your rotisserie motor. Check your device packaging for weight limits.

CLEANING, CARE, AND MAINTENANCE

It is critical to clean and care for your equipment regularly. Before starting, make sure your rotisserie rod is clean and that it fits correctly into the motor. After cooking, wash and wipe down the rod to remove any food residue before it gets a chance to start growing its own low and slow science experiment.

Throughout the cooking process, burning fats, charcoal, and wood smoke can leave behind a thick, black residue. Over time this build-up can flake off and land in your food, block vents, or sometimes disguise piles of grease and oil. It is good practice to periodically wash this buildup from the inside of your cooker. Your user manual will have instructions on the proper way to clean your equipment.

Using a cover for your grill is a great way to protect it from the elements and any critters freeloading in your backyard. But if you live in an excessively hot or cold region, you may want to store your cooker in a garage or shed.

If using a gas grill, make sure you have the gas hoses and mechanics checked regularly to ensure they are safe. Oh, and there is nothing worse than running out of propane midway through a cook, so here's a trick. Weigh your brand-new propane bottle when you get it home. Weigh it again when it's empty. Now, you'll always know how close you are to needing a refill.

Setting Up Your Grill Station

Preparation for barbecue begins by accumulating the necessary tools and equipment to make the best of your rotisserie. Have these items ready before igniting your grill.

› Basting brush and spray bottle

› Drip pan and water pan (see Making the Most of Your Drip Pan)

› Refrigerator packed with your favorite beverages, plus enough to share with a few people

› Heat-resistant gloves and tongs

› Heavy butcher's twine (see Trussing, page 9)

› Platters or aluminum foil trays to rest and serve food

› Sharp chef's knife and kitchen shears

› Spit forks and counterweights (see Preparing to Grill, page 14)

› Thermometer (like the Meater) to measure internal and ambient temperatures

MAKING THE MOST OF YOUR DRIP PAN

Drip pans are great for catching grease and other liquids that fall from your food as it rotates and cooks over the heat. Not only does using a drip pan prevent flare-ups and bitter smoke from ruining your food, but it is also a perfect way to collect drippings.

Your drip pan doubles as a water pan. The last thing you want is for your food to be drier than your dad's jokes. Using a water pan helps create a humid, moist environment inside your cooker, which results in tender, juicy food. You can use your imagination to introduce more flavor and complexity into your food; try using juice, stock, vinegar, or your favorite beverage in the pan, instead of plain water.

The Rotisserie Grill Kitchen

My philosophy of barbecue is that it should focus on common, easily available, fresh ingredients. Here are some items that show up repeatedly in my recipes.

PANTRY ESSENTIALS

I try to make sure I have all these ingredients tucked away for when the barbecue cravings come on strong.

- Apple cider vinegar
- Cayenne pepper
- Dried oregano
- Dried rosemary
- Dried sage
- Dried thyme
- Extra-virgin olive oil
- Garlic powder
- Granulated and light brown sugars, molasses, and honey
- Ground cinnamon
- Ground cumin
- Ground mustard
- Kosher salt: Morton's kosher salt is my go-to. If using a different salt with these recipes, you may need to adjust the quantities.
- Onion powder
- Paprika
- Red pepper flakes
- Your favorite hot sauce

REFRIGERATOR ESSENTIALS

As with pantry items, I try to keep my refrigerator fairly well stocked with items I know I will use often when rotisserie cooking.

- Apple juice
- Good-quality stocks and bone broths
- Ketchup
- Lemon and lime juice, or fresh lemons and limes

- Mayonnaise
- Minced garlic
- Soy sauce

- Unsalted butter
- Worcestershire sauce
- Yellow mustard

Trussing and Spitting Like a Pro

When it comes to rotisserie grilling, spitting the food correctly is critical. Spitting food on the grill involves piercing it with the long metal rotisserie rod—the spit—so the food can rotate while it cooks. Although the principle is simple, it can be difficult to execute properly. It's also important to know how to truss the food (tie the food snugly) correctly, so the food remains in place. By the end of this section, you will have an in-depth understanding of both techniques.

TRUSSING

To ensure that your food cooks evenly and consistently while it rotates (and doesn't fall off the rotisserie), you often have to truss, or bind, food together with twine before placing it on the rotisserie. Trussing involves tying food together snugly, so that the parts of the food that would otherwise hang closer to the fire are held together.

Trussing is most commonly used when cooking whole poultry, so the legs and wings can be held closer to the main body. Without trussing, the wings and legs would hang open and cook faster than the rest of the meat.

Trussing is also common with large pieces of meat that would otherwise be unsuitable for the rotisserie. Consider porchetta (see Crispy-Skinned Porchetta, page 72). Porchetta, generally made from pork belly, is filled with herbs and citrus. The pork belly is then rolled tightly and trussed, so it stays together throughout the cook. Without trussing, the pork belly would be unsuitable for the rotisserie, and all of the seasonings would be lost during rotation.

Always use heavy butcher's twine (not plastic twine!), which you can find in the baking section of your supermarket or at a local butcher shop. Here are step-by-step instructions on how to correctly truss poultry and roasts.

Chicken and Poultry

1. Place your whole chicken or other poultry, breast-side up, on a cutting board, and cut about 3 feet of heavy butcher's twine.

2. Place the twine under the back of the bird and slide it up until it is behind the wings, sitting just below the shoulder joints.

3. Draw the twine back toward the base of the breast and crisscross beneath the breast with the twine. As you do this, ensure you are drawing the string over the joint between the wingettes and the wing tip, so that, as you cross, the wings are pinned to the sides of the bird.

4. Using your crisscrossed twine, loop each end over both drumstick knuckles, drawing the thighs close to the base of the breast.

5. Flip the chicken over and cross the twine over the tail, pulling it tight before tying it off.

6. Double-knot your twine and cut off the excess.

7. You should be left with the chicken wings tightly bound to the body of the chicken, with the wing tips pinned in the space between the chicken thighs and the breast. Your drumsticks should be bound at the point where the twine meets at the base of the breast.

Roasts and Tenderloins

Whether you are trussing a bone-in or rolled roast, the steps and purpose of trussing are essentially the same.

1. Start by cutting pieces of string that are about twice as long as the circumference of the roast you are trussing. If you are trussing a bone-in roast, like a prime rib, cut enough pieces of twine to have at least one truss between each bone. If you are trussing a rolled roast, cut enough pieces of twine so you can tie a truss about every 2 inches.

2. Beginning in the center of the roast, loop one piece of twine around the joint, bringing the strings together and knot tightly. Hold the roast firmly together, until the knot is created. Trussing a rolled roast can take a little bit of practice, as you want to keep the meat tightly rolled before and during the trussing process.

3. Continue this process, looping and knotting, along the full length of the roast. You will know when it is complete and tight enough when you can drop the roast from a foot above your cutting board without losing any tightness in the knots.

SPITTING

Spitting is the act of skewering meat on a long rotisserie rod before placing it on the grill to slowly cook as it rotates over low heat. When spitting the meat, it is important to center the rod and balance the meat to help it cook evenly and avoid straining or damaging your rotisserie motor. A well-spit joint of meat will rotate evenly and consistently, allowing the slowly rendered fat and juices to baste the outside of the meat and developing an even caramelization across the food. Here are some step-by-step instructions.

Chicken and Poultry

1. Begin by placing your first rotisserie fork near the base of the rotisserie rod.

2. Assuming that you've already trussed your bird, slide the rotisserie rod through the cavity at the back, near the legs, and through the neck hole on the other side.

3. Slide your bird, legs first, down to the fork, until it is gently cradled in the prongs. The fork helps keep the bird in place, but depending on the design, it may not have to pierce the meat.

4. On the opposite end of the rotisserie rod, slide in your second fork, facing toward the chicken and cradling the neck/wing area between the fork prongs.

5. Push the rotisserie forks together, as much as possible, with the bird held securely between them. Focus on using the forks to keep the bird centered and balanced on the rotisserie rod.

6. Tighten the forks to the rods with the wing nuts.

Roasts and Tenderloins

1. Place your first rotisserie fork near the base of the rotisserie rod.

2. Slide the rotisserie rod lengthwise into the center of the trussed roast, from end to end. It's important to center the meat on the rod to keep balance and allow the rotisserie to spin easily.

3. Slide your roast down to the fork until it is gently cradled in the prongs. The fork helps keep the meat in place, but depending on the design, it may not have to pierce the meat.

4. Slide in your second fork, facing toward the roast, and cradle the meat between the prongs.

5. Push the rotisserie forks together, as much as possible, with the meat held securely between them.

6. Tighten the forks to the rods with the wing nuts.

ROTISSERIE GRILL HACKS

Now that you've mastered trussing and spitting meat, here are some pro tips to take your skills to the next level.

› **Consistent temperature.** The proteins in meat open and close depending on the temperature in the cooker. For best results, keep the ambient temperature inside the cooker consistent throughout the whole cook and your meat will be remarkably tender.

› **If you are looking, you ain't cooking.** Keep the lid on your rotisserie closed unless actively working on your food. Keep the heat in.

› **Resting your meat.** After a hard day's work, we all appreciate a little down time. Resting your meat will help it retain its juices and give the muscles a chance to relax, creating the ultimate in tender meat. Rest your meat at room temperature in an aluminum foil tray, loosely tented with foil.

› **Size and balance.** Keep your food as consistently sized and as centered as possible on the rotisserie to help it cook consistently and to help the rotisserie rotate evenly.

Cooking on the Rotisserie Grill

Now, it's time to get the fire going and make the final preparations.

PREPARING TO GRILL

Begin by setting your vents to the optimal position for the ambient temperature you want, and set up your rotisserie motor unit. The general rule is that the more open the vents, the hotter the temperature will become. You can adjust your vents throughout the cooking process, but it is easiest to do so now.

If using a rotisserie basket, attach it to your rotisserie rod before placing the rod into your cooker. Adding the basket onto a rod that has been sitting above the flames is like playing the worst game of hot potato imaginable.

If you are using a gas grill, skip ahead a paragraph, but for those working with charcoal, you definitely don't want to miss this part (and see All about Charcoal, page 15). For most cooks, set up your charcoal for indirect cooking and light your coals in a charcoal chimney. When the coals are about 70 percent covered in gray ash, place them into your cooker. If using smoking wood, add it now and close the lid on the grill. Let this burn for 20 to 30 minutes, until the smoke is no longer white and billowy but burning clean.

If cooking with a gas grill, set all the burners to high until you have met the desired ambient cooking temperature, then reduce the heat in your cooking zones to allow for indirect cooking. If you are going to cook with wood chips for smoke, add these 20 to 30 minutes before the food, so the smoke burns clean.

Now, insert the rotisserie rod into the rotisserie motor cradle. Switch on the rotisserie and watch for a couple of rotations to make sure it is spinning easily. If the rod is having a hard time turning or if it is spinning faster at some points of the rotation, you probably

ALL ABOUT CHARCOAL

If your cooker is set up for charcoal cooking, you have options and either style of charcoal will achieve good flavor and heat.

Charcoal briquettes are a compressed type of fuel made from wood by-products mixed with other ingredients and then pressed into regularly shaped briquettes. They are inexpensive, accessible, good for beginners, and easy to work with, but generally burn faster than lump and leave a lot of ash behind.

Lump charcoal is wood that has been slowly burned until all that is left is the carbon. Lump charcoal is well-known for being long-lasting and for leaving very little ash.

have a balance issue and need to check your trussing and spitting. If the balance still isn't right after you check and adjust, you may need to add some counterweights (small, heavy metal pieces that you can purchase separately) opposite the heavier parts of the meat, until it spins smoothly.

ON THE ROTISSERIE

Throughout the cook, make sure you regularly check and tend to your food, so your finished product has a nice crust, is super juicy, and is overflowing with flavor.

Basting: Basting adds great flavor, keeps food juicy, and builds a crust on the exterior of the meat. Similarly, you might spritz the meat with liquid in a spray bottle.

INCORPORATING WOOD CHIPS

Depending on the kind of cooker you are using, you can enhance the flavor of your food by incorporating wood smoke. Your local hardware store will usually sell you a smoke box for your gas/propane cooker, which allows you to burn wood chips as your meat cooks. If you are using charcoal, placing a piece of wood directly on the coals works.

When choosing wood, select the type of wood that makes the most sense for the type of meat you are cooking. Milder fruit woods are great for pork, poultry, and seafood, whereas hard woods, such as oak or hickory, are better for red meat.

Be careful not to oversmoke the food, and start to cook only after the smoke burns clean. Smoke should be used in the same way as salt and pepper. You want to add complexity to your food but not overpower the real flavor. A good guideline is to use wood about the size of your fist, but for fish or seafood, use half that amount.

Checking temperatures: Check the temperature of the meat and the ambient temperature of the cooker. Watch for situations where the temperature is increasing or decreasing quickly, because this is a sign of an issue (see Troubleshooting Like a Grill Master, page 22).

Meat placement: As meat cooks, it is common for the fibers to contract and move, meaning that meat that was perfectly balanced at the beginning of your cook might become bunched and the rotisserie might start struggling to turn. Watch for any balance issues, and if there are issues, switch off the rotisserie and adjust the meat so everything rotates smoothly.

WHEN IT'S DONE

After all the hard work you have put into the process of preparing and cooking the food (and explaining to your family why it takes twice as long to cook as it would if it was in the oven), it's important to treat it right before serving.

Because all meat is different, barbecue recipes aren't based on time but, rather, on temperature. Don't worry about how long the food has been cooking; focus on the temperature you are trying to reach. Make sure your thermometer is placed in the meat so it goes into the deepest, thickest parts but isn't touching bone or the rotisserie rod, which can throw off your reading. Make sure you understand your device.

Once your meat reaches your desired internal temperature, turn off the heat, remove the rotisserie rod from the cooker, and let your meat rest. Resting lets the fibers inside the meat relax and retain moisture when you slice into it. The more moisture the fibers can hold, the juicier your meat is.

The way you slice or carve meat can also affect its tenderness. All meat has fibers running through it, referred to as the grain. Imagine these lines as rubber bands. If you slice in the same direction that these rubber bands are running, you'll be chewing long, tough rubber bands. Alternatively, if you slice through the bands (against the grain), the pieces will be more tender and easier to eat.

ROTISSERIE GRILL TEMPERATURES AND COOKING TIMES

MEAT	DONENESS	INTERNAL TEMPERATURE IN DEGREES FAHRENHEIT	AMBIENT TEMPERATURE IN DEGREES FAHRENHEIT	APPROXIMATE TIME PER POUND
Beef brisket	Well-done	203 to 205	225 to 250	60 to 75 minutes per pound, plus rest time
Beef ribs	Well-done	203 to 205	225 to 250	60 to 75 minutes per pound, plus rest time
Beef roast	Rare	120	225 to 250	45 to 60 minutes per pound, plus rest time
	Medium	140	225 to 250	45 to 60 minutes per pound, plus rest time
	Medium-well	150	225 to 250	45 to 60 minutes per pound, plus rest time

MEAT	DONENESS	INTERNAL TEMPERATURE IN DEGREES FAHRENHEIT	AMBIENT TEMPERATURE IN DEGREES FAHRENHEIT	APPROXIMATE TIME PER POUND
Beef roast, pulled	Well-done	203 to 205	225 to 250	60 to 75 minutes per pound, plus rest time
Beef steak (reverse seared)	Rare	120	275 to 250	45 to 60 minutes per pound, plus sear
	Medium	140	275 to 250	45 to 60 minutes per pound, plus sear
	Medium-well	150	275 to 250	45 to 60 minutes per pound, plus sear
Chicken and poultry	Minimum safe	165	250 to 250	30 minutes per pound
Fish and seafood	Minimum safe	145	175	60 minutes per pound

MEAT	DONENESS	INTERNAL TEMPERATURE IN DEGREES FAHRENHEIT	AMBIENT TEMPERATURE IN DEGREES FAHRENHEIT	APPROXIMATE TIME PER POUND
Lamb chops/ steaks (reverse seared)	Rare	120	275 to 250	45 to 60 minutes per pound, plus sear
	Medium	140	275 to 250	45 to 60 minutes per pound, plus sear
	Medium-well	150	275 to 250	45 to 60 minutes per pound, plus sear
Lamb roast	Rare	120	225 to 250	45 to 60 minutes per pound, plus rest time
	Medium	140F	225 to 250	45 to 60 minutes per pound, plus rest time
	Medium-well	150	225 to 250	45 to 60 minutes per pound, plus rest time

MEAT	DONENESS	INTERNAL TEMPERATURE IN DEGREES FAHRENHEIT	AMBIENT TEMPERATURE IN DEGREES FAHRENHEIT	APPROXIMATE TIME PER POUND
Lamb roast, pulled	Well-done	203 to 205	225 to 250	60 minutes per pound, plus rest time
Pork, pulled	Well-done	203 to 205	225 to 250	60 minutes per pound, plus rest time
Pork ribs	Well-done	195 to 203	225 to 250	5 to 6 hours total
Pork roast, chops	Minimum safe	145	225 to 250	60 minutes per pound, plus rest time

TROUBLESHOOTING LIKE A GRILL MASTER

Regardless of how much experience you have as a cook, chef, or pitmaster, from time to time, unexpected things happen. Whatever the issue, what separates an average barbecuer from a grill master is how they handle these setbacks. For anything major, though, you may need to contact a professional.

PROBLEM	COMMON CAUSES	HOW TO FIX
Can't achieve ambient temperature	Vents blocked or not open correctly	Check your vents and clear away any material blocking air from passing through.
Temperature changing rapidly	Thermometer not placed correctly	For ambient temperatures, check that your temperature gauge or thermometer isn't touching anything inside the cooker, such as the meat or the water pan. For internal food temperatures, make sure that the thermometer probe is inserted into the food to the minimum depth and that it is not obstructed by anything inside the food, like the rotisserie rod or bones.
Food cooking inconsistently	Heat source is too direct	You may need to move the fuel or rotisserie rod to distance the food from the heat and allow it to cook more consistently.

PROBLEM	COMMON CAUSES	HOW TO FIX
Food is "slipping"	Trussing or rotisserie forks are not tight enough	Check that your trussing is still holding your food together tightly and that your forks are well positioned and tightened so your food continues to rotate.
Motor straining or being loud	Too much weight or unbalanced rotisserie	Check that the food is within the power limit of your rotisserie motor (see user manual) and that the weight is distributed evenly.
Bitter or overly smoked food	Wood not burning cleanly or too much wood	Let the wood burn for 20 to 30 minutes before placing food on the cooker. Check the smoke and avoid thick white or dark smoke. If smoke is running clean but your food is still bitter, you may be adding too much wood. You only need enough wood in the smoker for about the first 2 hours of the cook.
Rotisserie is not spinning	Rotisserie rod has slipped out of the collar	If your rotisserie is switched on, check to see if the collar is spinning. If the collar is spinning, switch it off temporarily and insert the rod back into the collar.

Blended Chimichurri **105**

About the Recipes

Now, it's time for my favorite tried-and-true rotisserie recipes. Some recipes, like Spit-Roasted Pineapple (page 31) or Picanha (page 81) are great options for beginners to get started. For those seeking more of a challenge, Crispy-Skinned Porchetta (page 72) could be just the recipe to give you that adrenaline rush and impress your guests.

Note that all recipes in this book can be cooked using both charcoal and gas cookers. Additionally, you are more than welcome to add wood for smoke, or you can cook without it. Each recipe specifies the amount of food you will be making, the prep time, the estimated cook time, ambient and internal temperatures, ingredients, and instructions. The recipes even include extra tips to help you get the best out of your food. Now, finally, it's time to fire up that grill.

CHAPTER 2

VEGETABLES, FISH, AND SEAFOOD

CAULIFLOWER BURNT ENDS

Serves: 2 to 4
Prep time: 20 minutes
Approximate cook time: 1 hour to 1 hour 15 minutes
Cooker temperature: 250°F, medium heat

Cauliflower burnt ends were made famous by LeRoy and Lewis Barbecue, a popular barbe-cue joint in Austin, Texas, and will thrill the vegetarian/vegan people in your life. This version uses harissa paste. Hailing from the northern parts of Africa, harissa paste combines chiles, citrus, peppers, and tomatoes to form a smoky, earthy, spicy marinade.

2 large red bell peppers

7 dried chipotle peppers (or your favorite pepper)

5 garlic cloves, peeled

¼ cup extra-virgin olive oil

Juice of 1 large lemon

2 tablespoons tomato paste

2 teaspoons ground coriander

2 teaspoons ground cumin

2 teaspoons smoked paprika

1 teaspoon fennel seeds

Pinch kosher salt

Pinch cracked black pepper

2 large heads cauliflower

Alabama White Sauce (page 102), for serving

1. Preheat the cooker to 250°F, medium heat.

2. Place the bell peppers directly onto or just above the fire for 10 to 15 minutes, until the skins become blistered and the flesh is tender. Blackening is fine but turn the pep-pers regularly to avoid burning the flesh. Let cool slightly, then remove the charred skins, stems, and seeds and place the bell pepper flesh in a blender or food proces-sor, along with the chipotle peppers, garlic, oil, lemon juice, tomato paste, coriander, cumin, paprika, fennel seeds, salt, and pepper. Blend until smooth to create the harissa. Set aside.

3. Remove the stems and exterior leaves from the cauliflower heads. Push the rotisserie rod through the base and out the top of the cauliflower heads before generously coat-ing them with the harissa. Place the rotisserie rod on the cooker and place a drip pan underneath.

4. Cook the cauliflower for 45 minutes to 1 hour, until it is tender, basting it every 15 min-utes with the harissa collected in the drip pan, coating all surface areas with the paste.

5. Right before removing the cauliflower from the heat, hold the cauliflower heads close to the fire to form a light to medium char across the surface, rotating them to ensure even coverage. Remove from the heat and break the heads into florets or "burnt ends."

6. Serve with the Alabama white sauce for dipping.

GRILLING TIP

As the cauliflower starts to soften and become tender, it has the potential to break away from the rotisserie rod. To avoid this, make sure you securely fasten it with rotisserie forks, and keep an eye out for potential breakages.

EMBERED POTATOES

Serves: 4 to 6
Prep time: 10 minutes
Approximate cook time: 1 hour 30 minutes
Cooker temperature: 350°F, high heat

Not many meals can't be improved by the addition of the humble potato, and rotisserie-style meats are no exception. This recipe is one I include pretty much every time I cook something on the spit. Here co-cooking is a must. By placing the potatoes directly beneath the spinning meat, they collect all of the incredibly delicious rendered fat and drippings from the meat, making these potatoes a crowd favorite.

2 pounds fingerling potatoes

3 tablespoons extra-virgin olive oil

2 tablespoons minced fresh rosemary leaves

1 tablespoon minced fresh parsley

2 teaspoons kosher salt

3 garlic cloves, minced

1 teaspoon cracked black pepper

3 tablespoons finely grated parmesan cheese

1. Preheat the cooker to 350°F, high heat.

2. Thoroughly wash the potatoes and place them in a disposable aluminum foil tray. Add the oil, rosemary, parsley, salt, garlic, and pepper to the tray and mix to coat the potatoes evenly. Place the tray underneath the rotisserie rod, where it can catch falling juices from whatever foods you are cooking above.

3. Cook for about 1 hour 30 minutes, stirring periodically, until the potatoes are tender. Ten minutes before removing them from the heat, sprinkle the parmesan cheese over the potatoes and allow it to warm. Serve the potatoes alongside your grilled meat.

GRILLING TIP

Make sure to account for the temperature of the heat so close to the fire. From time to time, you may need to adjust the position of the potatoes so they cook evenly.

SPIT-ROASTED PINEAPPLE

Serves: 4 to 6
Prep time: 10 minutes
Approximate cook time: 20 minutes
Cooker temperature: 250°F, medium heat

When I first moved to the United States, I found an amazing barbecue spot that was famous not for its meats but for its unique rotisserie pineapple. There is something about the sharp tartness of pineapple combined with the sweet, nutty smoke and brown sugar that makes this a truly memorable dessert. I have taken this concept and made it my own.

2 large whole pineapples

1 cup canned coconut cream

½ cup packed light brown sugar

1 tablespoon Tajín

2 teaspoons ground cinnamon

½ teaspoon ground cloves

1¼ cups heavy (whipping) cream

½ cup powdered sugar

1 teaspoon pure vanilla extract

1 cup mascarpone cheese

1. Preheat the cooker to 250°F, medium heat.

2. Remove the crown and rind from the pineapples and remove all of the eyes. Insert the rotisserie rod from the base to the top of each pineapple, securing them in place with the rotisserie forks. Lightly brush the coconut cream over the exterior of the pineapples to help the rub stick.

3. In a small bowl, stir together the brown sugar, Tajín, cinnamon, and cloves. Liberally coat the exterior of both pineapples. Place the spitted, seasoned pineapples onto the cooker for 15 to 20 minutes, until the rub becomes caramelized and sticky.

4. While the pineapple cooks, in a large bowl and using a handheld mixer, beat together the heavy cream, powdered sugar, and vanilla until soft peaks form. Add the mascarpone and whip until stiff peaks form.

5. Slice the pineapple tableside and serve with the mascarpone whipped cream.

SERVING TIP

To serve, slice off the exterior ½ inch of the pineapple, getting all of the amazing flavors you added to it—but don't think the rest of those pineapples is wasted! Brush the leftovers with more coconut cream and coat with more seasoning, then return the pineapple to the rotisserie to enjoy the second layer.

PESCADO ZARANDEADO ROTISSERIE BASKET

Serves: 4 to 6
Prep time: 20 minutes
Approximate cook time: 30 minutes
Cooker temperature: 300°F, medium-high heat
Internal temperature: 125°F to 130°F

The origins of this recipe go back more than 500 years to the western coast of Mexico. Traditionally, this recipe called for a white-fleshed fish, but I always use salmon because I can always find it fresh and affordable. In any event, the real magic of this dish comes from the way the fish is cooked. As the fish rotates, droplets of the mayonnaise fall into the fire, letting off a flavorful smoke that adds dimension and complexity to the fish, which is great served in a warm flour tortilla with your favorite toppings.

2 ancho chiles, stemmed and seeded
¼ cup mayonnaise
2 garlic cloves, finely chopped
2 tablespoons unsalted butter, melted
1 tablespoon soy sauce
1 tablespoon Worcestershire sauce
3 or 4 cilantro sprigs, roughly torn

Juice of ½ lime
Pinch kosher salt
Pinch cracked black pepper
1 large (3- to 4-pound) whole salmon, scaled, butterflied, head removed (ask your fishmonger to do this)

1. Tear the chiles into small flat pieces, about the size of a match head. In a medium bowl, combine them with the mayonnaise, garlic, melted butter, soy sauce, Worcestershire sauce, cilantro, lime juice, salt, and pepper. Stir to form the marinade.

2. Preheat the cooker to 300°F, medium-high heat.

3. Liberally and evenly slather the marinade across the meat side of the salmon. Place the salmon inside a rotisserie basket and place the basket immediately above the heat source so, as the fish drips, the heat creates that fragrant smoke.

4. Cook for about 30 minutes, until the salmon is pale pink and flaky and reaches an internal temperature of between 125°F and 130°F and the marinade has become caramelized and golden.

INGREDIENT TIP

When selecting the freshest salmon, look for clear, bright eyes and a shiny, slippery skin with no strong fish or ammonia-like odor.

BLACKENED FISH ROTISSERIE BASKET

Serves: 2 to 4
Prep time: 20 minutes
Approximate cook time: 20 minutes
Cooker temperature: 300°F, medium-high heat
Internal temperature: 155°F

Blackened fish may not look like the prettiest dish at the potluck, but what it lacks in looks, it makes up for in personality. Blackening as a technique originated in the French Quarter of New Orleans and has become a flagship feature for Creole-style cuisine. This recipe works well with some added wood smoke; use a subtle fruit wood, such as apple or cherry, but be careful not to oversmoke the food. Serve with a green salad and a wedge of lemon for squeezing over the fish.

2 teaspoons paprika
2 teaspoons garlic powder
1½ teaspoons kosher salt
1 teaspoon ground cumin
1 teaspoon dried thyme
½ teaspoon ground mustard
½ teaspoon ground white pepper

½ teaspoon dried oregano
½ teaspoon cayenne pepper
2 pounds firm-fleshed fish, filleted and skin removed (ask your fishmonger to do this; see Ingredient Tip)
8 tablespoons (1 stick) unsalted butter, melted, divided

1. Preheat the cooker to 300°F, medium-high heat.

2. In a medium bowl, stir together the paprika, garlic powder, salt, cumin, thyme, ground mustard, white pepper, oregano, and cayenne.

3. Brush all sides of the fillets with melted butter (reserve some for basting), and then coat them with the spice rub. Gently pat the rub to help it adhere to the fish.

4. Place the coated fillets inside the rotisserie basket and place the rotisserie rod on the cooker. Place a water pan underneath the fish.

5. Cook for 15 to 20 minutes, periodically basting the fish with the remaining melted butter, until the fish is flaky and tender and reaches an internal temperature of 155°F.

INGREDIENT TIP

Depending on where you live, your options for fish will vary. Search for a firm-fleshed fish like grouper, halibut, mahi mahi or, snapper.

THAI-STYLE SHRIMP ROTISSERIE BASKET

Serves: 2 to 4
Prep time: 5 minutes
Approximate cook time: 20 minutes
Cooker temperature: 225°F, low heat

Thai cuisine is characterized by its commitment to balancing sweet, sour, spicy, and bitter flavors to create dishes that touch all parts of the palate. Using the rotisserie for this recipe allows the balanced flavors to meld, infuse the meat evenly, and let the flavor of the shrimp shine. The bonus is that this recipe is particularly quick to make.

FOR THE RUB AND SHRIMP

4 teaspoons paprika

2 teaspoons ground turmeric

2 teaspoons cracked black pepper

2 teaspoons ground coriander

2 teaspoons ground ginger

2 teaspoons mustard seed

1 teaspoon ground mustard

1 teaspoon ground cumin

1 teaspoon cayenne pepper

4 pounds raw shrimp, peeled and deveined

FOR THE DIPPING SAUCE

½ cup fish sauce (like Dynasty brand)

Juice of 3 limes

¼ cup sugar

5 bird's-eye (or other preferred) chiles, diced

4 garlic cloves, minced

2 shallots, minced

2 teaspoons minced peeled fresh ginger

2 cilantro sprigs, finely minced

1. **To make the rub and shrimp:** In a small bowl, stir together the paprika, turmeric, black pepper, coriander, ginger, mustard seed, ground mustard, cumin, and cayenne until well combined. Place the rub in a zip-top bag, then add the shrimp. Seal the bag and gently shake to ensure the shrimp are evenly coated with the rub.

2. Preheat the cooker to 225°F, low heat.

3. Place the shrimp inside the rotisserie basket and place the rotisserie rod on the cooker. Place a water plan underneath the shrimp to help keep the cooker moist. If using smoke, add a subtle fruit wood, but don't oversmoke the food.

4. Cook for 15 to 20 minutes, or until the shrimp are C-shaped and the color is opaque (see Grilling tip). Shrimp do not take long to cook (overcooked shrimp are chewy), so keep an eye on them.

5. **To make the dipping sauce:** While the shrimp cook, in a medium bowl, whisk the fish sauce, lime juice, sugar, chiles, garlic, shallots, ginger, and cilantro to create a thin sauce for dipping.

GRILLING TIP

Watch your shrimp with a keen eye. Shrimp that have curled into a tight O shape are overcooked, whereas C-shaped shrimp are cooked perfectly. When the flesh becomes opaque with some pink and red sections, the shrimp are cooked.

SHRIMP PO'BOY ROTISSERIE BASKET

Serves: 2 to 4
Prep time: 10 minutes, plus 5 minutes to rest
Approximate cook time: 20 minutes
Cooker temperature: 225°F, low heat

Po'boy (short for "poor boy") sandwiches originated in the early 1900s during a streetcar workers' strike in Louisiana. These sandwiches were served free of charge in support of the striking workers and have become a Cajun staple. Po'boys are now made with ingredients ranging from roast beef to chicken, but are still most commonly filled with shrimp. My recipe steers away from the traditional breaded and deep-fried shrimp, instead including a smoky richness from smoked shrimp.

FOR THE RUB AND SHRIMP

2 tablespoons extra-virgin olive oil
1 tablespoon dried oregano
1 tablespoon dried thyme
2 teaspoons paprika
2 teaspoons cracked black pepper

2 garlic cloves, minced
1 teaspoon kosher salt
¼ teaspoon cayenne pepper
2 pounds raw shrimp, peeled and deveined

FOR THE CAJUN AÏOLI AND SANDWICH

½ cup mayonnaise
2 teaspoons freshly squeezed lemon juice
½ teaspoon paprika
½ teaspoon red pepper flakes
¼ teaspoon minced garlic

¼ teaspoon kosher salt
2 dashes hot sauce
4 to 8 French bread slices
Shredded lettuce, for serving
2 or 3 Roma tomatoes, diced

1. **To make the rub and shrimp:** In a medium bowl, stir together the oil, oregano, thyme, paprika, black pepper, garlic, salt, and cayenne. Gently stir in the shrimp and let it sit for a few minutes while you preheat the cooker.

2. Preheat the cooker to 225°F, low heat. If using smoke, add a subtle fruit wood, but don't oversmoke the food.

3. Place the shrimp in the rotisserie basket and place the rotisserie rod on the cooker. Place a water pan underneath the shrimp to help keep the cooker and shrimp moist.

4. Cook for 15 to 20 minutes, or until the shrimp are C-shaped and the flesh is opaque (see Thai-Style Shrimp Rotisserie Basket, Grilling tip, page 35).

5. **To make the Cajun aïoli and sandwich:** As the shrimp cook, in a small bowl, stir together the mayonnaise, lemon juice, paprika, red pepper flakes, garlic, salt, and hot sauce.

6. Remove the shrimp from the cooker and let rest for 5 minutes before piling them on the bread. Top with shredded lettuce, diced tomato, and Cajun aïoli. Serve immediately.

SERVING TIP

Toast your bread (butter it first) in a cast-iron skillet until golden. This adds wonderful texture to the sandwich and helps prevent it from getting soggy.

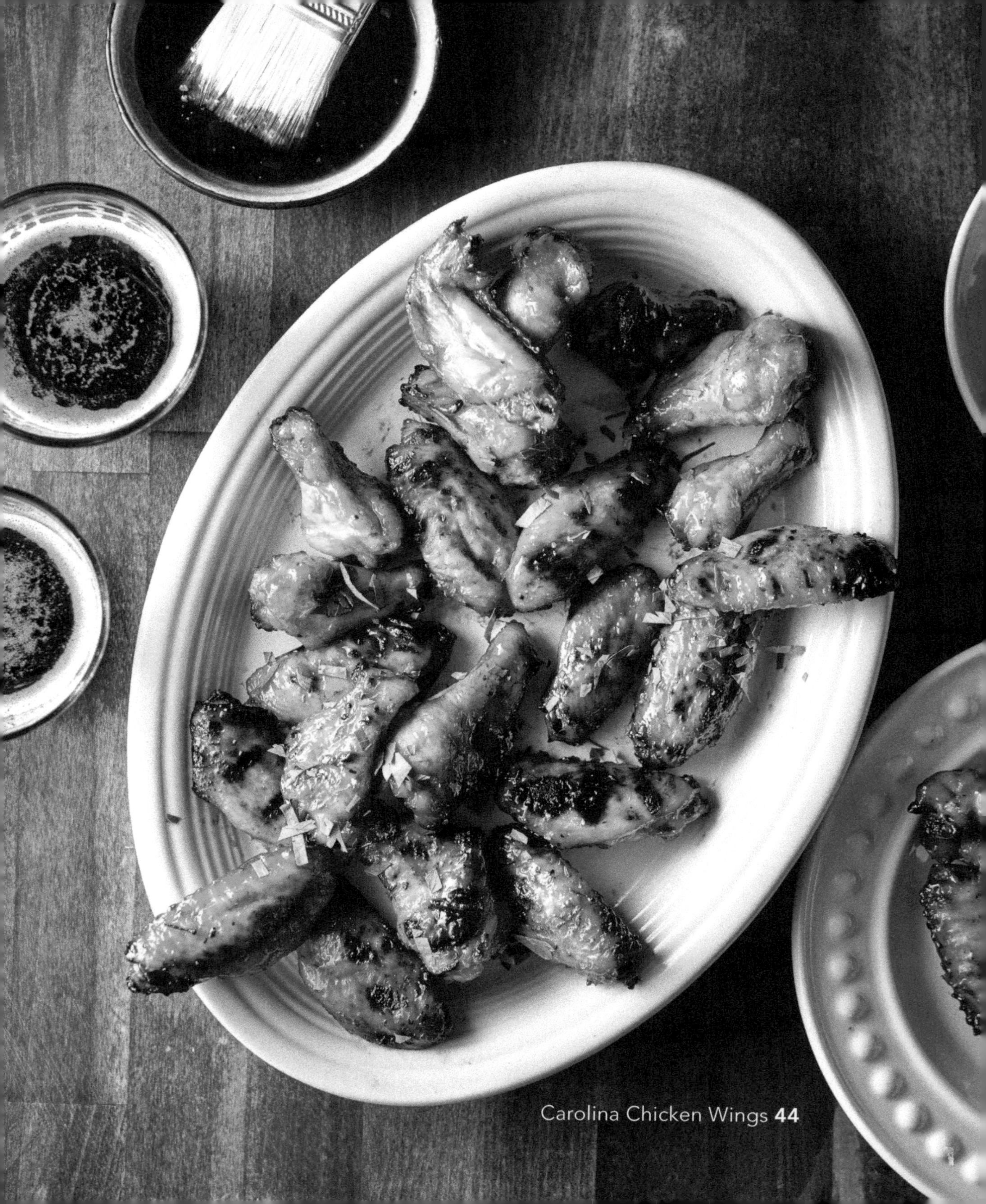

Carolina Chicken Wings 44

CHAPTER 3
POULTRY

TEXAS-STYLE MOPPED CHICKEN

Serves: 4 to 6
Prep time: 20 minutes, plus overnight to brine and 20 minutes to rest
Approximate cook time: 35 to 40 minutes per pound
Cooker temperature: 225°F, low heat
Internal temperature: 165°F

When it comes to rotisserie, chicken is, hands-down, the most popular protein. It's affordable, available, and versatile. But it can dry out easily. Mopping avoids this. Just as the name suggests, mopping is a technique that introduces liquid to the exterior of the chicken with a small mop, keeping the chicken juicy and developing amazing textures and flavors.

FOR THE BRINE, CHICKEN, AND RUB

2 "fryer" chickens
1 gallon Simple Brine (page 101)
1 cup All-Purpose Rub (page 103)
1 tablespoon paprika

2 teaspoons cayenne pepper
Alabama White Sauce (page 102) or ranch
    dressing, for serving

FOR THE MOP

2 cups apple cider vinegar
1 cup apple juice
¼ cup packed dark brown sugar
2 tablespoons cayenne pepper

1 tablespoon kosher salt
1 tablespoon cracked black pepper
1 tablespoon paprika
1 lemon, cut into ¼-inch slices

1. **To make the brine, chicken, and rub:** The day before you plan to serve the chicken, remove the spine of each chicken using a pair of sharp kitchen shears. Begin at the neck cavity and run the shears down either side of the spine. Flip the birds over and cut between the chicken breasts. You will find some resistance with the wishbone, but otherwise it is fairly easy to cut.

2. In a very large container, combine all four chicken halves with the brine, cover, and refrigerate overnight.

3. Preheat the cooker to 225°F, low heat.

4. Remove the chickens from the brine, wash them gently under cold water, and pat dry.

5. In a small bowl, stir together the rub, paprika, and cayenne and apply the rub liberally to all sides of the chickens. Place the chicken halves inside a rotisserie basket and place the rotisserie rod on the cooker. Let the chicken cook while you make the mop.

6. **To make the mop:** In a medium pot over medium-high heat on a stovetop, combine the vinegar and apple juice and heat until nearly boiling. Reduce the temperature to maintain a simmer and add the brown sugar, cayenne, salt, black pepper, paprika, and lemon slices. Stir until well incorporated and simmer for 5 minutes.

7. Cook the chicken, liberally applying the mop with a barbecue mop to all sides of the chicken about every 30 minutes, until it reaches an internal temperature of 165°F and turns a caramel-brown color on the outside.

8. Once the chicken is fully cooked, remove it from the cooker, loosely tent with aluminum foil, and let it rest for 20 minutes.

9. Serve with Alabama white sauce.

GRILLING TIP

Chicken meat is very subtly flavored, so it is important not to let it get overpowered by strong flavors. If you plan to use wood for smoking, use a mild fruit wood and make sure the smoke is clean before adding the food to the cooker.

TANDOORI CHICKEN

Serves: 4 to 6
Prep time: 20 minutes, plus overnight to marinate and 20 minutes to rest
Approximate cook time: 2 hours 30 minutes
Cooker temperature: 225°F, low heat
Internal temperature: 165°F

Traditional tandoori chicken gets its name (and juicy reputation) from the clay oven (tandoor) used frequently in Indian cooking. Luckily for those who do not have a tandoor, you can reach a similar outcome on the rotisserie, utilizing those same Indian-inspired flavors and carefully cooking the meat low and slow to get that same juicy, tender result.

2½ cups plain yogurt

3 tablespoons curry powder

3 tablespoons paprika

2 tablespoons minced garlic

1 tablespoon minced peeled fresh ginger

1 tablespoon cracked black pepper

1 tablespoon ground coriander

1 tablespoon ground cumin

1 tablespoon ground turmeric

2 teaspoons cayenne pepper

1½ teaspoons kosher salt

Juice of 1½ large lemons

1 bunch fresh cilantro leaves, finely chopped

12 boneless, skinless chicken thighs

1 large yellow onion, halved

1. In a large bowl, stir together the yogurt, curry powder, paprika, garlic, ginger, black pepper, coriander, cumin, turmeric, cayenne, salt, lemon juice, and cilantro. Set aside.

2. Using a sharp knife, score 2 or 3 parallel cuts into each chicken thigh, about ¼ inch deep, to help the marinade penetrate. Coat each thigh liberally with the marinade before piercing with the rotisserie rod. Place the chicken thighs (on the rod) on a baking sheet, cover, and refrigerate overnight.

3. Preheat the cooker to 225°F, low heat.

4. Place one onion half on each end of the rotisserie rod. Push the onion halves together to help condense the chicken thighs, then secure everything with rotisserie forks. Place the rotisserie rod on the cooker and place a water pan underneath. Cook the chicken for 2 to 2½ hours, until the internal temperature reaches 165°F and the chicken is a vibrant reddish orange beginning to char on the edges.

5. Remove the chicken from the cooker, loosely tent it with aluminum foil, and let rest for 20 minutes before serving.

SERVING TIP

Keep the chicken on the rotisserie rod and carve ½- to ¾-inch slices directly onto a plate. If needed, you can place the chicken over low heat to keep it warm while you eat.

CAROLINA CHICKEN WINGS

Serves: 2 to 4
Prep time: 10 minutes, plus overnight to brine and 15 minutes to rest
Approximate cook time: 1 hour 30 minutes
Cooker temperature: 250°F, medium heat

Low and slow barbecue is fueled by regional controversy. If you are in Texas, you insist on your cracked black pepper. If you are in Memphis, your ribs will have a dry rub but no sauce. The Carolinas have such a history of barbecue, and what they do in one spot is completely different from what they do in another. This chicken wing recipe is my interpretation of a North Carolina chicken wing, which includes a dry rub and a sauce with a spicy kick.

FOR THE WINGS

24 chicken wings
1 gallon Simple Brine (page 101)

Alabama White Sauce (page 102), for dipping

FOR THE RUB

¼ cup paprika
2 tablespoons granulated sugar
2 tablespoons light brown sugar
1 tablespoon kosher salt
1 tablespoon cracked black pepper

1 tablespoon ground white pepper
1 tablespoon ground cumin
2 teaspoons cayenne pepper
1½ teaspoons rubbed sage

FOR THE SAUCE

1½ cups apple cider vinegar
1 cup ketchup
¼ cup packed light brown sugar
3 tablespoons dark molasses
1 tablespoon honey

1 tablespoon kosher salt
1 tablespoon cracked black pepper
1 tablespoon red pepper flakes
2 teaspoons minced garlic

1. **To make the wings:** In a large container, combine the wings and brine, cover, and refrigerate overnight. Before cooking, remove the wings from the brine, gently rinse in cold water, and pat dry.

2. Preheat the cooker to 250°F, medium heat.

3. **To make the rub:** In a small bowl, stir together the paprika, granulated sugar, brown sugar, salt, black and white peppers, cumin, cayenne, and sage until well incorporated. Liberally coat each wing section with the rub (see Preparation tip).

4. Pierce each wing section with the rotisserie rod and place it onto the cooker. Place a water pan underneath the wings to catch drippings and help keep the wings juicy. Cook for 1 hour.

5. **To make the sauce:** While the wings cook, in a medium pot over medium-high heat on the stovetop, bring the vinegar nearly to a boil before reducing the heat to medium and allowing it to simmer. Stir in the ketchup, brown sugar, molasses, honey, salt, pepper, red pepper flakes, and garlic until well incorporated. Simmer the sauce for about 10 minutes, stirring frequently, until it becomes a deep brownish red and coats the back of a spoon.

6. After 1 hour of cooking, remove the wings from the rotisserie rod and dip each wing into the sauce. Gently shake off excess sauce but allow a thick layer to remain.

7. Place the wings back onto the rod and onto the cooker for another 30 minutes, until the sauce is tacky and sticky. Remove the wings from the heat and let them rest for 15 minutes before serving with Alabama white sauce for dipping.

• PREPARATION TIP

When adding the dry rub to the wings, don't cake too much on them. Because of the relatively short cook time, the rub won't break down very much and, if caked on, will leave a poor mouthfeel.

POLLO À LA BRASA

Serves: 4 to 6
Prep time: 15 minutes, plus 20 minutes to rest
Approximate cook time: 35 to 45 minutes per pound
Cooker temperature: 250°F, medium heat
Internal temperature: 165°F

Literally translating to "grilled chicken," pollo à la brasa is a popular Peruvian style of cooking chicken dating back to the 1950s. Originally reserved for high-end restaurants, these days, the dish is super popular and served just about everywhere. I fell in love with this recipe while living in Queensland, Australia, where it's commonly accompanied by fries and brown gravy. This recipe takes it back to the Peruvian style, serving it with aji verde, or "green sauce."

2 (3½- to 4½-pound) whole chickens

Embered Potatoes (page 30), for serving

FOR THE MARINADE

¼ cup paprika

¼ cup extra-virgin olive oil

2½ tablespoons kosher salt

2 tablespoons minced garlic

2 tablespoons white vinegar

1 tablespoon Dijon mustard

1 tablespoon freshly squeezed lime juice

1 tablespoon hot sauce

1 tablespoon ground cumin

2 teaspoons cracked black pepper

FOR THE AJI VERDE

1 cup fresh cilantro leaves

½ cup extra-virgin olive oil

¼ cup crumbled feta cheese

¼ cup mayonnaise

3 jalapeño peppers, seeded and diced

2 teaspoons chopped fresh oregano

2 teaspoons chopped fresh basil

2 garlic cloves, chopped

Juice of ½ lime

1 teaspoon kosher salt

1 teaspoon Dijon mustard

1 teaspoon honey

½ teaspoon white pepper

½ teaspoon ground cumin

1. Truss the chickens (see Trussing, Chicken and Poultry, page 10) and set aside.

2. Preheat the cooker to 250°F, medium heat.

3. **To make the marinade:** In a medium bowl, stir together the paprika, oil, salt, garlic, vinegar, Dijon, lime juice, hot sauce, cumin, and black pepper until well incorporated. Set aside.

4. Slide both chickens onto the rotisserie rod by inserting the rod through the neck cavity and out beneath the trussed chicken drums. Secure tightly with the rotisserie forks. Liberally coat each chicken with the marinade, making sure to get even and complete coverage. Place the rotisserie rod on the cooker. Place a water pan directly underneath the chickens to help keep them moist. Cook until each chicken reaches an internal temperature of 165°F and the skin has a caramel-brown color that is tacky to the touch.

5. **To make the aji verde:** While the chickens cook, in a blender or food processor, combine the cilantro, oil, feta, mayonnaise, jalapeños, oregano, basil, garlic, lime juice, salt, Dijon, honey, white pepper, and cumin and blend until smooth.

6. Once cooked, remove the chicken from the heat, loosely tent with aluminum foil, and let rest for 20 minutes. Carve the chicken into quarters and serve with aji verde and embered potatoes.

GRILLING TIP

Chickens tend to get off balance on the rotisserie. Ensure that the birds are trussed tightly, are well-balanced when placed on the rod, and that the rotisserie forks are well-secured and pushing the birds together tightly.

CHAR SIU DUCK

Serves: 4 to 6
Prep time: 15 minutes, plus 20 to 30 minutes to rest
Approximate cook time: 35 to 45 minutes per pound
Cooker temperature: 250°F, medium heat
Internal temperature: 165°F

Char siu (literally translated "fork roast" in Cantonese) is traditionally made with pork, but it also tastes amazing made with rich duck meat. Because of the high fat content in duck, particularly in duck skin, it is important to render the fat by scoring the skin. Scoring helps the skin crisp up nicely. Here, I opt for an easier route to achieve the traditional vibrant red color of this dish—red food coloring.

¼ cup hoisin sauce

¼ cup apple juice

2 tablespoons honey

2 tablespoons minced ginger

2 tablespoons soy sauce

1 tablespoon toasted sesame oil

1 tablespoon hot sauce

4 garlic cloves, minced

1 teaspoon Chinese five-spice powder

1 teaspoon red food coloring (optional)

1 (4- to 5-pound) whole duck

1. In a medium bowl, stir together the hoisin, apple juice, honey, ginger, soy sauce, sesame oil, hot sauce, garlic, five-spice powder, and food coloring (if using). Mix all of the ingredients into a thick marinade and apply it liberally across the whole duck. Pay special attention to the gaps between the wings and the body and the thighs and the body.

2. Using the tip of a sharp knife, score lines across the duck breast every ¼ inch to ½ inch. Ensure that your cuts are through the skin but not into the meat itself.

3. Preheat the cooker to 250°F, medium heat, and add cherry wood for smoke.

4. Place the duck on the rotisserie rod and secure it with the rotisserie forks. Place the rotisserie rod on the cooker and place a water pan underneath the duck. Cook until the breast reaches an internal temperature of 155°F and the skin is sticky and caramelized. During the cooking process, wrap the wings in foil if they are getting too dark.

5. At about 155°F internal temperature, ramp up the temperature of your fire to between 400°F and 450°F. This increased heat will help crisp the skin, render the fat, and bring the duck to the ideal internal temperature of 165°F. Loosely tent the cooked duck with aluminum foil and let rest for 20 to 30 minutes before slicing it the same way you would carve a chicken.

SERVING TIP

Some lightly pickled julienned cucumbers and carrots bring out the flavors of this dish beautifully. Or, serve with Chinese-style pancakes (or small tortillas).

ZESTY HERBED CHICKEN WITH BLACKBERRY SAUCE

Serves: 2 to 4
Prep time: 15 minutes, plus 20 minutes to rest
Approximate cook time: 35 to 45 minutes per pound
Cooker temperature: 250°F, medium heat
Internal temperature: 165°F

Chicken works with so many glazes and marinades, but to me, nothing beats a simple dry-rubbed bird. The rub for this recipe has a fair number of ingredients, but the combination of all those earthy and herby flavors combined with the acidity and brightness from the lemon makes my mouth water just thinking about it. Serve with a simple green salad to round out the meal.

FOR THE RUB, CHICKEN, AND SPRITZ

1 cup All-Purpose Rub (page 103)

2 tablespoons dried rosemary

2 tablespoons dried thyme

2 tablespoons dried basil

2 tablespoons dried marjoram

1 tablespoon ground fennel seed

1 tablespoon dried tarragon

2 teaspoons grated lemon zest (from 1 lemon)

1 (4- to 5-pound) whole chicken

1 cup water

Juice of 2 lemons

1 tablespoon sugar

FOR THE BLACKBERRY SAUCE

2 cups fresh blackberries

½ cup water

½ cup sugar

2 tablespoons apple cider vinegar

2 tablespoons blackberry preserves

Pinch ground nutmeg

1. Preheat the cooker to 250°F, medium heat. If you plan to use wood for smoking, use a mild fruit wood.

2. **To make the rub and prepare the chicken and spritz:** In a small bowl, stir together the rub, rosemary, thyme, basil, marjoram, fennel seed, tarragon, and lemon zest until well combined. Liberally and evenly coat the exterior of the chicken with the rub.

3. Tightly truss the chicken (see Trussing, Chicken and Poultry, page 10) and pierce it with the rotisserie rod, securing it tightly with the rotisserie forks.

4. In a spray bottle, make a simple spritz by combining the water, lemon juice, and sugar (see Preparation tip). Place the rotisserie rod on the cooker. Cook until the chicken reaches an internal temperature of 165°F, thoroughly spritzing the outside of the bird with the spritzing liquid every hour.

5. **To make the blackberry sauce:** While the chicken cooks, in a medium saucepan over medium heat on the stovetop, combine the blackberries, water, sugar, vinegar, preserves, and nutmeg. Cook, stirring, until well combined and simmering. Turn the heat to low and simmer the sauce for 10 minutes, stirring regularly.

6. Remove the cooked chicken from the cooker, loosely tent with aluminum foil, and let rest for 20 minutes before carving. Serve with the warm blackberry sauce.

PREPARATION TIP

Using a spritz when cooking chicken is a simple way to add extra juiciness and complexity to your chicken without brining it. A good spritz works best with a little bit of sugar to build color. Great spritz ingredients include apple cider vinegar, beer, fruit juice, soda, or stock.

ALABAMA WHITE CHICKEN ROTISSERIE BASKET

Serves: 4 to 6
Prep time: 25 minutes, plus overnight to brine and 10 minutes to rest
Approximate cook time: 2 hours
Cooker temperature: 250°F, medium heat
Internal temperature: 170°F

You might think you know what barbecue sauce is supposed to be—dark, sweet, and a little spicy—right? But Alabamians know that's just not true! Alabama white sauce is a delicious mayonnaise-based barbecue sauce that really ramps up the earthy and umami flavors in this chicken with its creamy, acidic flavor profile.

4 cups buttermilk
1½ tablespoons kosher salt
2 teaspoons cracked black pepper
12 chicken drumsticks
1 cup All-Purpose Rub (page 103)

2 tablespoons light brown sugar
1 tablespoon cayenne pepper
1 teaspoon ground turmeric
2 cups Alabama White Sauce (page 102),
  for serving

1. The day before you plan to cook, in a zip-top bag, combine the buttermilk, salt, and black pepper. Add the drumsticks and mix them around to coat. Seal the bag, removing all the air, and refrigerate overnight.

2. Right before cooking, remove the chicken from the brine, pat it dry, and discard the brine.

3. Preheat the cooker to 250°F, medium heat.

4. In a medium bowl, thoroughly mix the rub, brown sugar, cayenne, and turmeric. Coat the full exterior of each drumstick with the rub.

5. Enclose the drumsticks, top to tail, in a rotisserie basket and place the rotisserie rod on the cooker. Cook the chicken for about 2 hours, until it reaches an internal temperature of 170°F, being careful to avoid the bone when checking the temperature. The chicken will have a dark caramel color.

6. Let the drumsticks rest for 10 minutes, then serve with the Alabama white sauce.

● PREPARATION TIP

Soaking chicken overnight in buttermilk may not be traditional, but it does much of the work we look for from a traditional brine. The fat and acid in the buttermilk help break down the proteins so they become more tender, as well as allow the skin to crisp as the meat cooks.

THANKSGIVING TURKEY

Serves: 8 to 10
Prep time: 30 minutes, plus 2 hours to cool, 2 nights to brine, and 30 minutes to rest
Approximate cook time: 30 minutes per pound
Cooker temperature: 225°F, low heat
Internal temperature: 165°F

Growing up in New Zealand and, later, Australia, Thanksgiving was just something I knew about from TV. But when I moved to the States, I adopted it as my own; it epitomizes my philosophy of food and barbecue, which is that it is an opportunity for friends and family to gather, to share, to talk, and to enjoy something together. When you add that kind of experience to a holiday dedicated to showing gratitude, it makes for a perfect day.

FOR THE BRINE AND TURKEY

1 gallon Simple Brine (page 101; substitute apple cider for the apple juice)
6 whole cloves
2 Fuji apples, quartered
1 yellow onion, quartered
Peel of 1 orange
2 cinnamon sticks

2 rosemary sprigs
2 thyme sprigs
2 sage sprigs
1 tablespoon ground allspice
1 (12-pound) turkey, thawed if frozen
8 tablespoons (1 stick) unsalted butter, at room temperature

FOR THE RUB

1½ cups All-Purpose Rub (page 103)
2 teaspoons rubbed sage
2 teaspoons dried rosemary
2 teaspoons dried parsley flakes

1½ tablespoons light brown sugar
1 teaspoon ground ginger
1 teaspoon celery salt

FOR THE SPRITZ

8 tablespoons (1 stick) unsalted butter, melted   1 cup water

1. **To make the brine and prepare the turkey:** Two nights before Thanksgiving, in a large stockpot (that will fit the turkey), over medium-high heat on the stovetop, combine the brine, cloves, apples, onion, orange peel, cinnamon, rosemary, thyme, sage, and allspice. Bring the mixture to a boil and boil for 5 minutes, stirring constantly.

2. Let the brine cool fully, about 2 hours in the refrigerator, before adding the turkey and completely submerging it in the brine. Cover and refrigerate for 2 nights until ready to begin cooking.

3. Preheat the cooker to 225°F, low heat. If you plan to use wood for smoking, use a mild fruit wood like cherry and don't oversmoke the meat.

4. Remove the brined turkey, discard the brine, rinse the turkey, and pat it dry. Coat the entire surface of the turkey with the room-temperature butter, being mindful to get it in the gaps between the body and the wings and the body and the thighs.

5. **To make the rub:** In a medium bowl, stir together the rub, sage, rosemary, parsley, brown sugar, ginger, and celery salt until well incorporated. Thoroughly coat the buttered turkey with the rub, paying careful attention to the same gaps. Try to get the rub as even and smooth as possible.

6. Tightly truss your turkey (see Trussing, Chicken and Poultry, page 10) and place it onto a rotisserie rod, securing it tightly with the rotisserie forks. Turkeys are big and can be very heavy, so it may be a good idea to use a food-safe U-bolt (see tips) to secure the turkey to the rod, so it doesn't spin. Place the rotisserie rod on the cooker and place a drip pan underneath.

7. **To make the spritz:** In a spray bottle, combine the melted butter and water. Every hour while cooking, spritz or baste the turkey with the mixture.

8. Cook the turkey until the thighs reach an internal temperature of 165°F and the turkey has a dark caramel color. Remove the turkey from the heat, loosely tent with aluminum foil, and let rest for 30 minutes before carving. As the meat rests, use the drippings to make a gravy, or as the liquid for your stuffing. You'll thank me later.

INGREDIENT AND GRILLING TIPS

If your turkey has been frozen, ensure that you allow enough time for it to thaw before you cook it: at least 2 to 3 days in the refrigerator before adding it to the brine. Large turkeys can be a challenge to fasten securely to a rotisserie rod. Try using a simple trussing U-bolt. The U-bolt is looped around the rotisserie rod inside the turkey, pushed through the turkey on either side of the spine, then the wing nuts are tightened. Be sure to check for balance and utilize counter-weights as needed (see Preparing to Grill, page 14).

UNCONVENTIONAL JERK CHICKEN

Serves: 2 to 4
Prep time: 20 minutes, plus overnight to marinate and 20 minutes to rest
Approximate cook time: 30 minutes per pound
Cooker temperature: 225°F, low heat
Internal temperature: 165°F

Here's your chance to enjoy some flavors of the Caribbean, no passport required. I love the unexpected spices, like allspice, cinnamon, and nutmeg. Somewhere during the cooking process, when those spices, the Scotch bonnets, and the scallions all get to know each other, magic melds them into an astounding flavor. My recipe strays from the traditional; it uses root beer instead of rum and ground allspice rather than allspice berries. This jerk chicken is delicious with a simple cilantro-lime rice and your favorite mango salsa.

4 garlic cloves, minced

2 Scotch bonnet peppers, seeds and stems included

1 bunch scallions, white and pale green parts only, roughly chopped

1 red onion, chopped

2 tablespoons chopped fresh thyme

1 tablespoon ground allspice

1 tablespoon ground cinnamon

1 tablespoon ground nutmeg

1 tablespoon ground ginger

2 teaspoons cracked black pepper

½ cup root beer

Juice of 1 lime

¼ cup soy sauce

2 tablespoons molasses

1 tablespoon Worcestershire sauce

1 (4- to 5-pound) whole chicken, butterflied (see Preparation tip)

1. The night before you cook, in a food processor, combine the garlic, peppers, scallions, red onion, thyme, allspice, cinnamon, nutmeg, ginger, and pepper. Pulse lightly to combine. While pulsing regularly, add the liquids one a time: root beer, lime juice, soy sauce, molasses, and Worcestershire sauce, pulsing until you have a coarse paste.

2. Generously coat all sides of the chicken with the paste, then place it in a large zip-top bag. Seal the bag, pressing out all the air, and refrigerate overnight.

3. Preheat the cooker to 225°F, low heat.

4. If you have butterflied the chicken, place it in a rotisserie basket. Otherwise, truss the chicken tightly (see Trussing, Chicken and Poultry, page 10) and pierce it with a rotisserie rod, securing it with the rotisserie forks.

5. Wrap the basket (if using) or the chicken tightly in aluminum foil and cook, covered, for 1½ to 2 hours, until the chicken reaches an internal temperature of about 110°F. Remove the foil, add a water pan, and continue to cook, uncovered, until the chicken reaches an internal temperature of 165°F.

6. Loosely tent the chicken with aluminum foil and let rest for 20 minutes before carving and serving.

PREPARATION AND INGREDIENT TIPS

This recipe lends itself well to butterflying or spatchcocking the chicken, or you can cook the bird whole. Note that Scotch bonnets pack lots of heat, so if spice isn't your thing, remove the seeds, or replace them with milder jalapeño peppers.

GARLIC AND CITRUS CHICKEN

Serves: 2 to 4
Prep time: 15 minutes, plus overnight to marinate and 20 minutes to rest
Approximate cook time: 35 to 45 minutes per pound
Cooker temperature: 250°F, medium heat
Internal temperature: 165°F

When it comes to the incredible versatility of chicken, this healthy, tangy recipe is a show-stopper. Incorporating herbs, juices, honey, and oil, this marinated chicken recipe ticks all the taste boxes. It is also insanely easy to make; you literally mix everything in a food processor or bowl before slathering it on the chicken and letting it marinate.

½ cup freshly squeezed orange juice

4 garlic cloves, minced

Grated zest of 2 lemons

Juice of 2 lemons

1 tablespoon Dijon mustard

1 tablespoon extra-virgin olive oil

1 tablespoon honey

2 teaspoons grated orange zest (from 1 orange)

2 shallots, finely diced

1 teaspoon dried oregano

1 teaspoon dried thyme

1 teaspoon kosher salt

1 teaspoon cracked black pepper

1 (4- to 5-pound) whole chicken

1. In a food processor or blender, combine the orange juice, garlic, lemon zest, lemon juice, Dijon, oil, honey, orange zest, shallots, oregano, thyme, salt, and pepper and process until well incorporated. The texture of the marinade should be like a runny, textured honey.

2. Pour the marinade into a shallow dish and coat the full exterior of the chicken with it. Cover and place in the refrigerator overnight. A couple of times while the chicken marinates, baste it with the marinade. While it sits, the marinade may start to separate, so give it a quick stir first.

3. Preheat the cooker to 250°F, medium heat.

4. Tightly truss your chicken (see Trussing, Chicken and Poultry, page 10), reserving the marinade, before inserting the rotisserie rod and securing it with the rotisserie forks. In a medium saucepan over high heat, bring the reserved marinade to a boil, then boil for 1 minute.

5. Place the rotisserie rod on the cooker and place a drip pan underneath. Fill the pan with the boiled marinade. Baste the chicken every 45 minutes with the marinade and juices collected in the drip pan.

6. Once the chicken is a golden mahogany brown and the chicken thighs reach an internal temperature of 165°F, remove it from the cooker, loosely tent with aluminum foil, and let rest for 20 minutes before carving and serving.

PREPARATION TIP

When zesting citrus fruit, be careful to get only the exterior colored skin, not the bitter white pith underneath.

SATAY CHICKEN ROTISSERIE BASKET

Serves: 2 to 4
Prep time: 20 minutes, plus 15 to 20 minutes to rest
Approximate cook time: 2 hours
Cooker temperature: 225°F, low heat
Internal temperature: 165°F

Originating in Indonesia, but claimed by so many different cultures, chicken satay is the perfect blend of earthy, spicy, sweet, and umami flavors. For convenience, this recipe strays a bit from tradition, using some easier-to-find ingredients, like peanut butter, but it is no less delicious. The introduction of smoke brings extra complexity to the dish that you can't achieve in the oven. A fresh cucumber or green salad makes a lovely accompaniment.

FOR THE MARINADE AND CHICKEN

⅔ cup canned coconut milk

¼ cup freshly squeezed lime juice (from about 2 limes)

2 tablespoons soy sauce

2 tablespoons light brown sugar

2 garlic cloves, minced

1 tablespoon smoked paprika

2 teaspoons kosher salt

2 teaspoons ground turmeric

½ cup extra-crunchy peanut butter

4 large (1½ to 2 pounds total) bone-in, skinless chicken thighs

2 teaspoons red pepper flakes

FOR THE PEANUT DIPPING SAUCE

½ cup extra-crunchy peanut butter

3 tablespoons apple cider vinegar

3 tablespoons honey

2 tablespoons soy sauce

1 teaspoon minced garlic

Coconut milk, for thinning

1. **To make the marinade and prepare the chicken:** In a large bowl, whisk the coconut milk, lime juice, soy sauce, brown sugar, garlic, paprika, salt, and turmeric until well incorporated. Using a mixing spoon, stir the peanut butter into the coconut milk mixture until it is thin enough to whisk until well combined.

2. Preheat the cooker to 225°F, low heat.

3. Dip the chicken thighs into the satay marinade and rub gently to help the marinade adhere to the chicken. Sprinkle all sides with the red pepper flakes.

4. Place the marinated chicken thighs inside a rotisserie basket and place the rotisserie rod on the cooker. Cook for 1½ to 2 hours, until the thighs reach an internal temperature of at least 165°F and they become a golden brown-orange color with some charring on the edges. Remove and let rest for 15 to 20 minutes.

5. **To make the peanut dipping sauce:** While the chicken rests, in a medium bowl, whisk the peanut butter, vinegar, honey, soy sauce, and garlic until blended. To reach your desired consistency, add some coconut milk or water as you whisk. Serve the chicken with the dipping sauce.

GRILLING TIP

The bones release a lot of flavor while cooking but, when testing for doneness with the thermometer, be careful not to hit the bone or you'll risk a false temperature read.

Blackberry-Glazed Pork Ribs **76**

CHAPTER 4

PORK

CRISPY-SKINNED PORK BELLY BURNT ENDS

Serves: 4 to 6

Prep time: 20 minutes, plus overnight to salt and 15 minutes to rest

Approximate cook time: 4 hours 30 minutes

Cooker temperature: 250°F, medium heat

Internal temperature: 200°F

Burnt ends are traditionally sliced from the fatty part of a brisket. Although less traditional, the high fat content inside a pork belly is so similar to brisket that it makes a comparable morsel of meat candy. With just a few simple ingredients, this recipe takes what would be a normal delicious pork belly burnt end and creates a masterpiece slab with a thick, glassy layer of crispy pork skin on top.

1 (6- to 8-pound) skin-on pork belly

½ cup kosher salt

1 cup All-Purpose Rub (page 103)

1 cup Blackberry Glaze (page 106)

1 tablespoon extra-virgin olive oil

1. The day before you cook, score parallel lines into the pork belly skin, about 1 inch apart. Be careful to cut only through the skin and not into the fat. Salt the skin heavily (save a bit of salt for dusting) and refrigerate overnight, skin-side up, uncovered, on a wire rack.

2. Preheat the cooker to 250°F, medium heat.

3. Pat the pork skin dry with a paper towel. Flip the pork belly skin-side down and cut deep slices almost to the skin but without penetrating it. Cuts should run from side to side and be about 1 inch apart.

4. Turn the pork belly 90 degrees and cut from side to side again, about 1 inch apart. You should now have 1-by-1-inch squares across your pork belly, with one side still attached to the skin. Season the meat side of your pork belly liberally with the rub, working to get the rub inside the cuts.

5. Place the pork belly into a rotisserie basket and place the rotisserie rod on the cooker. Cook until the pork reaches an internal temperature of 200°F.

6. Glaze the meat side of the pork belly liberally with the blackberry glaze, getting the sauce between the cracks of the pork. Apply a light layer of oil to the skin side of the pork belly and liberally dust with the remaining salt.

7. Now, ramp up the temperature of your fire to high heat, about 450°F, and stop the rotisserie basket spinning when the pork is skin-side toward the fire.

8. Keep a close eye on the pork skin as the crackling forms. The skin will bubble and become a light-yellow color. If needed, move the pork belly so the crackling forms consistently. Some edges may brown, but don't let the crackling burn. This should take 10 to 15 minutes.

9. Once the crackling has formed, transfer the pork belly to a wire rack, skin-side up, and let it rest for 15 minutes.

10. To slice, cut through the crackling, following the cuts made before it was cooked. You should now be left with 1-by-1-inch cubes of sticky pork belly, with a thick top of crispy crackling.

INGREDIENT TIP

When selecting pork belly, look for a 50:50 fat to meat ratio. Find a pork belly with a consistent thickness across, which will help you get an even cook.

MUSTARD AND APRICOT HAM

Serves: 10 (with plenty left over for sandwiches)
Prep time: 30 minutes, plus 30 minutes to rest
Approximate cook time: 50 minutes to 1 hour per pound
Cooker temperature: 225°F, low heat
Internal temperature: 200°F

Where I grew up, ham was a luxury, so it was something we truly looked forward to at Christmas. My mum would always make the same mustard glaze, and whatever wasn't eaten on the big day, we were thrilled to use in sandwiches over the next few. This recipe is my twist on my mum's. To this day, the smell reminds me of Christmas day swims (remember, Southern Hemisphere) and delectable leftovers.

1 (8- to 9-pound) uncooked bone-in ham

¾ cup Dijon mustard, plus more for the surface layer

1 cup All-Purpose Rub (page 103)

1 tablespoon cracked black pepper

¾ cup apricot preserves

1 tablespoon apple cider vinegar

1 tablespoon light brown sugar

1. Using a sharp knife, score a diamond pattern across the surface of the ham; cut through the skin, but less than ¼ inch deep.

2. Rub a light layer of Dijon across the full surface of the ham, before generously coating it with the rub and pepper.

3. Preheat the cooker to 225°F, low heat.

4. Place the ham, flat-side down, on a work surface and insert the point of the rotisserie rod into the meat, close to the bone. Use a small rubber mallet to drive the rod through the meat. Secure the rod with rotisserie forks and place rotisserie rod on the cooker. Place a water pan underneath the ham. Cook the ham for 1½ hours.

5. While the ham cooks, in a medium bowl, stir together the Dijon, preserves, vinegar, and brown sugar to form a glaze.

6. After 1½ hours, empty the water pan and place it back in the cooker. Baste the full exterior of the ham with the glaze. Every 1½ hours or so, baste the whole ham with the drippings in the drip pan, adding some water if they're too thick.

7. Once the ham reaches an internal temperature of 165°F, wrap it tightly in aluminum foil and continue to cook until it reaches an internal temperature of 200°F. Then, remove the foil, baste the ham with any lost glaze in the drip pan, and let it cook for 5 minutes more.

8. Remove the ham from heat, loosely tent with aluminum foil, and let rest for 30 minutes. Carve the ham into ¼-inch slices and serve your incredibly grateful guests.

SERVING TIP

When slicing ham, start from the outside and work your way in. You can reglaze any leftover ham with the mustard and apricot mixture and place it back on the rotisserie, or in the oven, for about 30 minutes until the glaze sets.

CIDER-BRINED PORK CHOPS

Serves: 6
Prep time: 10 minutes, plus overnight to brine and 15 minutes to rest
Approximate cook time: 45 minutes to 1 hour
Cooker temperature: 250°F, medium heat
Internal temperature: 145°F

Rotisserie-style cooking lends itself to big joints of meat, but that doesn't mean you can't cook things that are already portioned into individual servings. These pork chops are juicy, flavorful, simple to serve crowd-pleasers. After all, there is a reason pork is the most eaten meat in the world.

2 large Fuji or similar apples, cored and quartered
1 gallon Simple Brine (page 101; replace the apple juice with apple cider)
6 large (¾- to 1-inch-thick) pork chops

¾ cup All-Purpose Rub (page 103)
1 teaspoon celery salt
2 cups water
2 cups apple cider

1. In a medium bowl, combine the apples and brine. Put the pork chops in, cover, and refrigerate overnight to brine.

2. When ready to cook, remove the pork chops from the brine, lightly rinse with cold water, and pat them dry.

3. Preheat the cooker to 250°F, medium heat.

4. In a small bowl, stir together the rub and celery salt. Apply the rub liberally to all sides of the pork chops.

5. Truss the pork chops together before piercing them with the rotisserie rod close to the bone, then secure them with rotisserie forks. Place the rotisserie rod on the cooker.

6. Fill a water pan with the water and cider and place it underneath the pork.

7. Cook the pork until it reaches an internal temperature of 145°F, then remove it from the cooker. Loosely tent with aluminum foil and let rest for 15 minutes, before removing the trussing and serving.

● INGREDIENT TIP

When selecting pork chops, look for chops with a consistent shape and fat content. This will help them cook more seamlessly together.

BARBECUE PORK BUTT

Serves: 6 to 8
Prep time: 5 minutes, plus 30 minutes to rest
Approximate cook time: 30 to 40 minutes per pound
Cooker temperature: 225°F, low heat
Internal temperature: 155°F

Despite what the name suggests, the pork butt comes from the pig's shoulder. Pork butt is frequently used for pulled pork because it is readily available, affordable, and can feed a lot of people. Serve with apple sauce and Embered Potatoes (page 30) for a complete meal. You thought I was going to make a cheeky, butt-related joke, didn't you?

¾ cup packed light brown sugar
½ cup sweet paprika
¼ cup kosher salt
3 tablespoons garlic powder
2 tablespoons cracked black pepper
2 tablespoons onion powder

2 tablespoons dried rosemary
1 (6- to 7-pound) bone-in pork shoulder (see Preparation tip)
1 cup apple juice
1 cup water

1. In a medium bowl, stir together the brown sugar, paprika, salt, garlic powder, pepper, onion powder, and rosemary until well incorporated. Liberally coat the exterior of the pork butt with this rub.

2. Preheat the cooker to 225°F, low heat.

3. Insert the rotisserie rod through the center of the pork butt, being mindful of the shoulder bone. Secure it with the rotisserie forks. Place the rotisserie rod on the cooker and place a drip pan underneath.

4. Fill a spray bottle with the apple juice and water. After the first 2 hours, begin spritzing the pork every hour with the mixture.

5. Cook the pork until it reaches an internal temperature of 155°F. Remove it from the heat, loosely tent with aluminum foil, and let rest for 20 to 30 minutes.

6. Slice the pork against the grain into ¼-inch slices.

PREPARATION TIP

Pork butt generally has a thick fat cap across the top of the joint. Trim this fat down to about ¼ inch, so that as the pork cooks, the fat adds flavor and moisture but also has a chance to render so it's not rubbery.

TRADITIONAL PORK LOIN ROAST

Serves: 6 to 8
Prep time: 20 minutes, plus overnight to brine and 20 minutes to rest
Approximate cook time: 1 hour 10 minutes
Cooker temperature: 225°F, low heat
Internal temperature: 145°F

Pork loin roast is a lean joint of meat that runs through the back of the pig. It is the spot from which the pork chop is cut. It is more heart healthy, but the downside is that its lack of fat makes it dry out easily. So, be careful not to overcook this recipe; pay close attention to the internal temperature and do not let the pork get hard.

1 (4- to 5-pound) boneless pork loin roast
1 gallon Simple Brine (page 101)
6 garlic cloves, minced
¼ cup fresh rosemary leaves
2 tablespoons fennel seeds
½ cup All-Purpose Rub (page 103)

1 teaspoon cayenne pepper
¼ cup maple syrup
1 tablespoon apple cider vinegar
1 tablespoon Dijon mustard
1 tablespoon grated lemon zest

1. The day before cooking, truss your roast into a log shape, beginning in the middle, with trusses every 2 inches (see Trussing, Roasts and Tenderloins, page 11). This will help the roast cook evenly and maintain its shape.

2. In a very large bowl, stir together the brine, garlic, rosemary, and fennel seeds. Submerge the roast in the brine, cover, and refrigerate overnight.

3. Preheat the cooker to 225°F, low heat.

4. Remove the roast from the brine, lightly rinse it under cold water, and pat dry. Liberally coat the pork with the rub and cayenne, before inserting the rotisserie rod and securing it with the rotisserie forks. Place the rotisserie rod on the cooker and place a water pan underneath.

5. As the pork cooks, in a small bowl, stir together the maple syrup, vinegar, Dijon, and lemon zest.

6. When the pork reaches an internal temperature of 140°F (nearly finished cooking), brush the full exterior of the meat with the maple glaze.

7. Continue to cook the pork for about 5 minutes more, or until it reaches 145°F, before removing it from the cooker. Loosely tent the pork with aluminum foil and let rest for 20 minutes. Slice the pork into ¼- to ½-inch-thick slices against the grain and serve.

INGREDIENT TIP

Fennel seed has an almost licorice flavor and smell, which adds interesting complexity to the other ingredients in this dish.

CRISPY-SKINNED PORCHETTA

Serves: 6 to 8
Prep time: 30 minutes, plus overnight to marinate and 30 minutes to rest
Approximate cook time: 35 to 45 minutes per pound
Cooker temperature: 225°F, low heat
Internal temperature: 145°F

Originating in Italy, this dish is now made with a wide variety of ingredients using a range of techniques. Traditionally, porchetta was made from a loin roast, but I prefer to use pork belly for that perfect ratio of fat to meat. Step it up a notch and serve porchetta as a sandwich with crusty bread, stone-ground mustard, and arugula for a real treat.

1 (7- to 8-pound) whole boneless, skin-on
   pork belly
10 garlic cloves, finely minced
1 cup roughly chopped toasted pine nuts
2 tablespoons plus ½ cup kosher salt, divided
2 tablespoons cracked black pepper
2 tablespoons whole fennel seeds
1 tablespoon red pepper flakes

1 tablespoon ground nutmeg
3 rosemary sprigs, chopped
3 sage sprigs, chopped
Juice of 1 lemon
Juice of 1 orange
Grated zest of 1 lemon
Grated zest of 1 orange
1 tablespoon canola oil

1. Prepare the belly for marinating by trimming the edges into straight lines. This will make it much easier to roll. Note that any skin inside the rolled belly is going to become rubbery. So, to avoid this, roll the belly up, scoring the skin to indicate the section contained inside the roll. Unroll and remove this section of skin.

2. Score the remaining skin about 1 inch apart across the meat side of the pork belly, cutting just through the skin but not into the meat or fat. Place the pork belly, skin-side down, and make side to side ½-inch-deep cuts across the full length of the belly, about 1 inch apart. Turn the pork belly 90 degrees and complete the same cuts side to side. You should now have a checkerboard effect of 1-by-1-inch squares across the belly.

3. Evenly layer the garlic, pine nuts, 2 tablespoons of salt, pepper, fennel seeds, red pepper flakes, nutmeg, rosemary, sage, lemon juice, and orange juice across the meat side of the belly. Sprinkle the lemon zest and orange zest across the meat.

4. Roll the porchetta like a roll of wrapping paper (the ends will look like a spiral) and, using butcher's knots (see Preparation tip), truss the roll tightly about every 2 inches.

5. Place the trussed porchetta on a wire rack and sprinkle ¼ cup of salt liberally across the full surface of the skin. Place the belly, uncovered, in the refrigerator overnight.

6. Preheat the cooker to 225°F, low heat.

7. Pat the pork skin dry with a paper towel to remove any moisture. Lightly brush the oil across the skin, before coating it with the remaining ¼ cup of salt.

8. Place the porchetta on the spit and secure it with the rotisserie forks. Place the rotisserie rod on the cooker and cook until the pork reaches an internal temperature of 145°F. As the pork gets close to temperature, ramp up the temperature of your fire to between 450°F and 500°F to crisp the skin for about the last 20 minutes. Pork crackling will blister and bubble as it forms, so keep an eye on it to prevent burning.

9. Remove the porchetta from the cooker, loosely tent it with aluminum foil, and let rest for 30 minutes before slicing and serving.

PREPARATION TIP

A search on YouTube will reveal some great options for tying butcher's knots but, ultimately, all that matters is that your knots keep the trussing in place. Use any knot that will work.

MOJO PORK

Serves: 6 to 8
Prep time: 15 minutes, plus 32 to 36 hours to brine and marinate and 30 minutes to rest
Approximate cook time: 35 to 40 minutes per pound
Cooker temperature: 225°F, low heat
Internal temperature: 165°F

A few years ago, I watched an amazing movie about a passionate chef starting a food truck. He highlighted a Cuban sandwich made with mojo pork. Mojo is a Cuban style of pork featuring lots of fresh herbs and citrus. At the time, I was just getting into smoking and decided to try my hand at Cuban sandwiches, but with an extra smoke twist. What resulted is still one of my favorite recipes ever. Make the mojo into an incredible but simple toasted sandwich with Swiss cheese, yellow mustard, and pickles.

1 (6- to 8-pound) boneless pork shoulder

FOR THE BRINE

4 cups freshly squeezed orange juice

2 cups water

½ cup rice wine vinegar

½ cup kosher salt

¼ cup packed light brown sugar

2 or 3 oregano sprigs, coarsely chopped

2 or 3 rosemary sprigs, coarsely chopped

2 or 3 sage sprigs, coarsely chopped

3 bay leaves

1 garlic head, crushed, cloves separated
  and peeled

FOR THE MARINADE

½ cup extra-virgin olive oil

½ cup chopped fresh cilantro

¼ cup chopped fresh mint

2 tablespoons chopped fresh oregano

2 tablespoons ground cumin

1 garlic head, crushed, cloves separated
  and peeled

Grated zest of 3 oranges

Juice of 3 oranges

Grated zest of 6 limes

Juice of 6 limes

1. Trim the skin and excess fat from the pork shoulder. I like to cut scores 1 to 2 inches deep throughout the pork shoulder, so both the brine and marinade can penetrate better.

2. **To make the brine:** In an extra-large zip-top bag, combine the orange juice, water, vinegar, salt, brown sugar, oregano, rosemary, sage, bay leaves, and garlic. Add the pork shoulder. If the shoulder is especially large, cut it in half, and do this process in two bags. Seal the bag and refrigerate the pork overnight, flipping the bag to ensure even coverage.

3. Remove the pork from the brine. Rinse it under cold water and pat dry.

4. **To make the marinade:** In a food processor or blender, combine the oil, cilantro, mint, oregano, cumin, garlic, orange zest, orange juice, lime zest, and lime juice. Process until blended and smooth. Transfer the marinade to an extra-large zip-top bag and add the brined pork. Seal the bag and refrigerate to marinate for at least 8 hours.

5. Preheat the cooker to 225°F, low heat. If you plan to use wood for smoking, use a mild fruit wood, like cherry.

6. Place the pork shoulder on the rotisserie rod and secure it with the rotisserie forks. Place the rotisserie rod on the cooker and place a drip pan underneath.

7. Cook the pork, basting it every hour with the dripping marinade, until it reaches an internal temperature of 165°F. Remove the pork from the smoker, loosely tent it with aluminum foil, and let rest for 30 minutes, before slicing into ¼- to ½-inch-thick slices to serve.

PREPARATION TIP

Traditional Cuban sandwiches are cooked on a plancha—a very hot metal plate used for searing. Alternatively, they are cooked in a cast-iron skillet with something heavy sitting on top (like another skillet). This helps keep the sandwich together while cutting and eating it.

BLACKBERRY-GLAZED PORK RIBS

Serves: 2 to 4
Prep time: 10 minutes, plus 15 to 20 minutes to rest
Approximate cook time: 5 hours
Cooker temperature: 225°F, low heat

To this day, pork ribs are one of my favorite things to smoke and cook on the rotisserie, even though doing so requires a little creativity to get the spit in place. The finished product is even more tender, delicious, and memorable than when cooked flat on a smoker.

2 racks baby back pork ribs

¾ cup packed dark brown sugar, divided

1 tablespoon kosher salt

1 tablespoon smoked paprika

2 teaspoons cracked black pepper

2 teaspoons garlic powder

2 teaspoons onion powder

1 teaspoon ground cumin

2 cups apple juice

4 tablespoons (½ stick) butter, cut into
   ¼-inch pieces

2 cups Blackberry Glaze (page 106)

1. Remove the silver skin from the back of the ribs.

2. In a medium bowl, stir together ¼ cup of brown sugar, the salt, paprika, pepper, garlic powder, onion powder, and cumin to form a dry rub. Liberally apply the rub to all sides of the pork ribs.

3. Preheat the cooker to 225°F, low heat.

4. Truss both racks of pork ribs together very tightly, bone to bone, with trussing about 2 inches apart. Slide the rotisserie rod between the trussed ribs from end to end before securing it with the rotisserie forks. Place the rotisserie rod on the cooker and place a water pan underneath. Cook the ribs for 3 hours. During this time, the ribs are going to darken in color and the exterior meat is going to begin to firm up and become tacky to the touch.

5. After 3 hours, remove the ribs from the cooker, leaving the rod in place, and place them on a double layer of aluminum foil pieces that are 24 inches long. Turn the edges of the foil up to create a vessel. Sprinkle ¼ cup of brown sugar across each rack and add the apple juice and butter slices to the foil vessel.

6. While keeping the liquid contained, wrap the ribs tightly in the foil before wrapping a third layer of foil around the whole package. Ensure that the foil is well wrapped, particularly around the rotisserie rod. Place the foil-wrapped ribs back onto the cooker for 1 hour.

7. After 1 hour, remove the ribs from the cooker and very carefully remove the foil from the ribs. Using a basting brush, liberally coat the ribs with the blackberry glaze and return them to the cooker, uncovered, for about 1 hour, until the glaze is sticky and well set.

8. Remove the rotisserie rod and cut the trussing. Place the ribs on a cutting board, bone-side down, to rest for 15 to 20 minutes before slicing and serving.

INGREDIENT TIP

Baby back ribs typically come in a standard size, about 5 inches wide and with 11 or 12 ribs per rack. Look for the thickest, meatiest ribs with the most consistent size.

Churrasco-Style Tri-Tip 90

BEEF AND LAMB

MOROCCAN LAMB LOLLIPOPS

Serves: 4 to 6
Prep time: 10 minutes, plus 15 minutes to rest
Approximate cook time: 30 to 45 minutes
Cooker temperature: 225°F, low heat
Internal temperature: 145°F

If you know anything about New Zealand, you know its people are crazy about lamb. This recipe for a Moroccan-style lamb is one of my favorites and is a true crowd-pleaser. Serve it with couscous, dried cranberries, chickpeas, roasted red onions, roasted carrots, and a nice sharp yogurt dressing and you will be in paradise.

2 garlic cloves, minced

2 tablespoons chopped fresh mint

2 tablespoons chopped fresh cilantro

1 tablespoon fennel seeds

2 teaspoons smoked paprika

2 teaspoons ground cumin

1 teaspoon sugar

½ teaspoon ground cardamon

½ teaspoon cayenne pepper

Juice of ½ lemon

8 lamb cutlets

Garlic Yogurt Sauce (page 100), for serving

1. In a medium bowl, stir together the garlic, mint, cilantro, fennel seeds, paprika, cumin, sugar, cardamom, cayenne, and lemon juice until a coarse paste forms. Spread the paste over the full surface of the lamb cutlets.

2. Preheat the cooker to 225°F, low heat.

3. If you plan to use wood for smoking, lamb can hold up to some good hard woods like pecan or hickory. Pierce the lamb cutlets through the center of each with the rotisserie rod and secure the group with rotisserie forks. Place the rotisserie rod on the cooker.

4. Cook the lamb until it reaches an internal temperature of 145°F (USDA recommended) or your desired doneness. Medium-rare, which I prefer, is an internal temperature of 125°F. I find that cooking lamb more than medium-rare increases its gaminess and dries it out.

5. Remove the lamb from the heat, loosely tent with aluminum foil, and let rest for 15 minutes before serving. Serve with the garlic yogurt sauce.

INGREDIENT TIP

Lamb chops are generally bigger and come from the shoulder. Cutlets come from the loin. Look for lamb cutlets with a bright red color and a nice fat cap, ¼ to ½ inch, running down one side.

PICANHA

Serves: 6 to 8
Prep time: 15 minutes
Approximate cook time: 35 minutes
Cooker temperature: 450°F, high heat
Internal temperature: 145°F

Also called the rump cap or sirloin cap, picanha is a large, difficult-to-cook joint of meat, recognizable by its large thick fat cap across one side. Picanha was first made popular in Brazil, and what it lacks in tenderness it makes up for in flavor. Its large fat cap makes it perfect for rotisserie cooking because, as it rotates, it self-bastes to add even more flavor to the meat. Serve with Cauliflower Burnt Ends (page 28) and Blended Chimichurri (page 105) for an incredible flavor experience.

1 (3- to 4-pound) picanha
2 tablespoons extra-virgin olive oil
¼ cup kosher salt

2 tablespoons cracked black pepper
2 tablespoons garlic powder
1 teaspoon ground mustard

1. Using a sharp knife, slice the picanha *with* the grain into individual steaks, about 1½ to 2 inches thick. Do not remove or trim the fat cap. Fold each steak into a C shape with the fat cap facing out and pierce with the rotisserie rod to maintain this shape. You should be able to fit 2 or 3 steaks on the rod before securing it with rotisserie forks.

2. Preheat the cooker to 450°F, high heat.

3. Using a basting brush, lightly coat the exterior of the steaks, including the fat cap, with oil.

4. In a medium bowl, stir together the salt, pepper, garlic powder, and ground mustard and generously and evenly coat the exterior of each steak with the rub.

5. Place the rotisserie rod on the cooker and place a water pan underneath. Cook the picanha until it reaches an internal temperature of 145°F (USDA recommended) or your desired doneness. Medium-rare, which I prefer, is an internal temperature of 125°F to 130°F.

6. Serve picanha tableside, carving ¼-inch-thick slices directly onto the plate. If needed, picanha can be re-seasoned and placed back on the cooker to develop a further crust.

PREPARATION TIP

Place the raw meat in the freezer for 20 minutes before slicing. This will firm up the meat and make it much easier (and safer) to slice as desired.

HERB-CRUSTED BEEF TENDERLOIN

Serves: 2 to 4
Prep time: 10 minutes, plus 20 minutes to rest
Approximate cook time: 40 to 50 minutes per pound
Cooker temperature: 225°F, low heat
Internal temperature: 145°F

For beef that's more tender than a mother's love, it is hard to beat the delectable beef tenderloin. Tenderloin is an oblong-shaped, non-working muscle, generally considered to be the most tender meat on the cow. In fact, filet mignon is cut from the beef tenderloin. Cooking tenderloin on the rotisserie is a great way to prevent it from drying out because the juices expelled from the meat have a second life basting the meat's exterior. Your favorite root vegetables make a delicious accompaniment.

1 (4-pound) center-cut beef tenderloin

1 tablespoon extra-virgin olive oil

1 tablespoon kosher salt

1 tablespoon cracked black pepper

1 tablespoon finely diced fresh parsley

1 tablespoon finely diced fresh basil

1 tablespoon finely diced fresh thyme

2 teaspoons garlic powder

1. Begin by trussing the beef tenderloin about every inch along the body of the joint (see Trussing, Roasts and Tenderloins, page 11). Lightly coat the exterior of the tenderloin with the oil to act as a binder.

2. In a medium bowl, stir together the salt, pepper, parsley, basil, thyme, and garlic powder. Evenly coat the full tenderloin with the spice mixture.

3. Preheat the cooker to 225°F, low heat.

4. Pierce the tenderloin with the rotisserie rod through the center of the joint, keeping the rod as central as possible, and secure it with the rotisserie forks. Place the rotisserie rod on the cooker and place a water pan in the cooker to raise the moisture level and juiciness of the beef. Cook the tenderloin until it reaches an internal temperature of 145°F (USDA recommended) or your desired doneness. Medium-rare, which I prefer, is an internal temperature of 125°F to 130°F.

5. Remove the tenderloin from the heat, loosely tent with aluminum foil, and let rest for 20 minutes.

6. Return the tenderloin to the cooker, directly above the heat source without activating the rotisserie function. Sear each side for about 1 minute, until a crust forms. Serve immediately.

GRILLING TIP

Reverse searing is a technique used to cook meat (usually beef) first to an internal doneness, then searing it quickly on the outside to develop a crust.

BEEF SHORT RIB REUBEN

Serves: 6 to 8
Prep time: 30 minutes, plus 2 hours to cool, 10 days to cure, and 1 hour to rest
Approximate cook time: 1 hour per pound
Cooker temperature: 225°F, low heat
Internal temperature: 203°F

You shouldn't ever leave New York City without trying a classic Reuben sandwich. Dating back to 1908, the Reuben is an incredible combination of textures and flavors, the hero being juicy, succulent pastrami beef. Traditional pastrami is made with a beef brisket and is often steamed or roasted. Introducing the rotisserie and smoking, as well as using beef ribs here, may stray from the traditional preparation—but it is worth it.

FOR THE BRINE AND BEEF

1 gallon water
1 cup kosher salt
¾ cup packed light brown sugar
1 tablespoon Worcestershire sauce
1 tablespoon mustard seeds
2 teaspoons coriander seeds
2 teaspoons Prague powder #1 (meat curing salt)

8 whole cloves
5 juniper berries, crushed
5 garlic cloves, crushed
3 bay leaves
2 cinnamon sticks
2 (3½-pound) short rib racks

FOR THE RUB

½ cup cracked black pepper
½ cup coriander seeds
1 tablespoon mustard seeds
1 tablespoon garlic powder

1 tablespoon paprika
1½ teaspoons granulated sugar
Extra-virgin olive oil or yellow mustard,
   for coating (optional)

1. **To make the brine and cure the beef:** In a large stockpot, combine the water, salt, brown sugar, Worcestershire sauce, mustard seeds, coriander seeds, Prague powder, cloves, juniper berries, garlic, bay leaves, and cinnamon sticks. Bring to a simmer over medium-high heat on the stovetop and let simmer for 10 minutes, stirring thoroughly. Set aside to cool completely, about 2 hours in the refrigerator, before adding the beef.

2. Using a sharp knife, aggressively trim the thick fat cap and the silver skin beneath it from the ribs, leaving only the beef exposed. Add the short ribs to the cooled brine, cover, and refrigerate to cure the beef for 10 days, flipping every other day to ensure even brine coverage.

3. Once the beef has cured and you are ready to cook, remove it from the brine and gently rinse with cold water, then pat dry with paper towels. The beef will have an anemic gray tinge, but this is normal.

4. Preheat the cooker to 225°F, low heat.

5. **To make the rub:** In a medium bowl, stir together the pepper, coriander seeds, mustard seeds, garlic powder, paprika, and sugar. Generously coat the outside of the meat on all sides with the rub. If needed, rub the meat with some oil or mustard first to act as a binder to help the rub stick.

6. Place the ribs, bone-side together so the bones are touching, before trussing tightly. Insert the rotisserie rod between the trussed ribs and secure it with the rotisserie forks. Place the rotisserie rod on the cooker. If you plan to use wood for smoking, use a fist-size piece of cherry wood to add great sweet flavor.

7. Cook the ribs until they reach an internal temperature of 203°F, spritzing every hour with water to help develop a thick, firm bark.

8. Remove the ribs from the cooker, loosely tent with aluminum foil, and let rest for 1 hour. The ribs will be soft and tender, so you can easily remove the bones and shred the meat, similar to pulled pork.

SERVING TIP

This meat can stand alone but comes into its element when served as a sandwich. Traditional fillings include sauerkraut, Thousand Island dressing, and Swiss cheese, all placed between slices of rye bread.

GREEK MARINATED LAMB

Serves: 8 to 10
Prep time: 10 minutes, plus 4 to 6 hours to marinate and 1 hour to rest
Approximate cook time: 35 minutes per pound
Cooker temperature: 225°F, low heat
Internal temperature: 145°F

There is something about traditional Greek flavorings of fresh herbs, lemon juice, and olive oil that just work so well with lamb. The citrus in this marinade helps cut some of the lamb's gamey flavor, and the simple Garlic Yogurt Sauce (page 100) highlights the unique, complex flavors of the lamb itself.

1 (6- to 8-pound) bone-in leg of lamb

4 large garlic cloves, partially crushed

¼ cup extra-virgin olive oil

1 tablespoon finely chopped fresh oregano

1 tablespoon finely chopped fresh thyme

2 teaspoons kosher salt

1 teaspoon cracked black pepper

Grated zest of 1 lemon

Juice of 1 lemon

Garlic Yogurt Sauce (page 100), for serving

1. Using a sharp knife, trim off any thick fat (leave about ¼ inch) or any visible silver skin that could become chewy as the lamb cooks.

2. In a small bowl, 4 to 6 hours before cooking, stir together the garlic, oil, oregano, thyme, salt, pepper, lemon zest, and lemon juice. Pour this marinade into a large zip-top bag and add the lamb. Seal the bag, removing as much air as possible. Massage the marinade across the lamb's surface. Refrigerate for 4 to 6 hours. At about the halfway point, flip the lamb and massage the marinade into the lamb again.

3. Preheat the cooker to 225°F, low heat.

4. Remove the lamb but retain the marinade. Pierce the lamb leg with the rotisserie rod, placing the rod as close to the bone as possible, balancing the lamb as best as possible on the rod. Secure it with the rotisserie forks.

5. In a medium saucepan over high heat, bring the reserved marinade to a boil, then boil for 1 minute.

6. Place the rotisserie rod on the cooker and place a drip pan underneath.

7. While cooking, baste the lamb regularly with the reserved marinade and pan drippings. Cook until the lamb reaches an internal temperature of 145°F (USDA recommended) or your desired doneness. Medium-rare, which I prefer, is an internal temperature of 125°F. I find that cooking lamb to more than medium-rare increases its gaminess and dries it out.

8. Once the lamb reaches temperature, remove it from the cooker, loosely tent with aluminum foil, and let rest for 1 hour, before slicing the meat against the grain and serving with the yogurt sauce.

PREPARATION TIP

Before cooking, make six 1- to 1½-inch-deep incisions across the surface of the lamb. Place a peeled garlic clove in each incision and press firmly so it stays in place. These garlic cloves help flavor the meat and become part of the slices as you carve the lamb.

BEEF SHORT RIBS

Serves: 4 to 6
Prep time: 20 minutes, plus 1 hour to rest
Approximate cook time: 45 minutes to 1 hour per pound
Cooker temperature: 225°F, low heat
Internal temperature: 203°F

If you love pork ribs, beef ribs are about to change your life. Often referred to as brisket on a stick, beef ribs bring the best of both brisket and ribs to the party. Similar to a brisket, beef ribs are a working muscle, so they need to be cooked low and slow to become tender. Unlike a brisket, beef ribs contain a lot of marbled fat, making them uniquely delicious.

2 (3-pound) beef short ribs
1½ cups Charcoal Beef Rub (page 107)
1½ cups beef stock, divided

½ cup apple cider vinegar
½ cup water

1. Remove the thick fat cap entirely from the short ribs and the underlying silver skin. Unlike pork ribs, removing the membrane from the back of beef ribs isn't necessary.

2. Preheat the cooker to 225°F, low heat.

3. Generously and evenly coat all sides of the beef ribs with the rub, including the bones, before tightly trussing the beef ribs back-to-back with the bones pressed together. Insert the rotisserie rod between the two racks and secure it with the rotisserie forks. Place the rotisserie rod on the cooker. Fill a water pan with 1 cup of stock and place it underneath the short ribs, before closing the lid. Cook the beef ribs for 2 hours.

4. In a spray bottle, combine the remaining ½ cup of stock, the vinegar, and water. After the first 2 hours, spritz the beef ribs every hour to help develop a thick, delicious bark.

5. Once the ribs reach an internal temperature of 203°F, remove them from the cooker, loosely tent with aluminum foil, and let rest for 45 minutes to 1 hour.

6. Slice the beef ribs between the bones and serve. The beef should be juicy, tender, and easily bitten from the bone, without falling apart.

INGREDIENT TIP

Beef ribs come in two main types: short ribs and back ribs. Raw short ribs have about 1 inch to 1½ inches of meat in between. Beef back ribs like a rack of pork spareribs.

BRAAI T-BONE ROTISSERIE BASKET

Serves: 4
Prep time: 10 minutes, plus 20 minutes to rest
Approximate cook time: 1 hour
Cooker temperature: 225°F, low heat
Internal temperature: 145°F

Nearly every culture has its version of barbecue. Some, like Korean or American, may be more well known than others, but around the world there are amazing things going on. Take South African braai. A braai is similar to a barbecue in that it uses fire/coals to cook meat. But one of my favorite things about it is, even after the food is cooked, the fire is maintained, so guests can gather around it. This recipe for T-bones is a riff on traditional braai-cooked meats, featuring their typical abundant spices and flavors. Serve with traditional barbecue sides like potato salad and baked beans.

¼ cup kosher salt

2 tablespoons light brown sugar

2 tablespoons ground coriander

2 tablespoons paprika

1 tablespoon ground cumin

1 tablespoon cracked black pepper

1 tablespoon garlic powder

1 tablespoon onion powder

1 tablespoon dried thyme

1 teaspoon cayenne pepper

1 teaspoon allspice

4 (at least 1-inch-thick) T-bone steaks

1. In a medium bowl, stir together the salt, brown sugar, coriander, paprika, cumin, black pepper, garlic powder, onion powder, thyme, cayenne, and allspice until thoroughly mixed. Coat all sides of the T-bones with the dry rub.

2. Preheat the cooker to 225°F, low heat.

3. Place the seasoned T-bones inside a rotisserie basket, keeping the edges from touching or overlapping as much as possible. Place the rotisserie rod on the cooker and cook until the T-bones reach an internal temperature of 145°F (USDA recommended) or your desired doneness. Medium-rare, which I prefer, is an internal temperature of 125°F. Remove the steaks from the heat, loosely tent with aluminum foil, and let rest for 15 to 20 minutes.

4. Return the steaks to the cooker directly above the heat source. Sear each side for 1 to 2 minutes, until a thick crust forms.

CHURRASCO-STYLE TRI-TIP

Serves: 4 to 6
Prep time: 15 minutes, plus overnight to marinate and 20 minutes to rest
Approximate cook time: 35 minutes per pound
Cooker temperature: 225°F, low heat
Internal temperature: 145°F

Churrasco is a Brazilian style of barbecue that usually involves cooking proteins on long metal skewers above an open fire or embers. It highlights simple flavors and ingredients, allowing the flavor of the meat and the fire to shine. Here, you'll use tri-tip steak, which is a tender, triangular cut of beef that hails from the lower part of the sirloin. Complete the feast with Blended Chimichurri (page 105) and Embered Potatoes (page 30).

2 (2- to 3-pound) tri-tip steaks
½ cup freshly squeezed orange juice (from 2 or 3 oranges)
¼ cup freshly squeezed lime juice (from about 2 limes)
2 tablespoons soy sauce
2 tablespoons extra-virgin olive oil

2 tablespoons garlic powder
2 tablespoons onion powder
2 tablespoons kosher salt
1 tablespoon paprika
1 tablespoon cracked black pepper
1½ teaspoons ground cumin
½ teaspoon cayenne pepper

1. Remove any silver skin from the tri-tips, along with any large pockets of thick fat (leave about ¼ inch) that won't render while cooking.

2. In a food processor, combine the orange juice, lime juice, soy sauce, oil, garlic powder, onion powder, salt, paprika, black pepper, cumin, and cayenne and blend until smooth. Pour the marinade into a large zip-top bag and add the trimmed tri-tips. Seal the bag, removing all the air from the bag. Massage the marinade into the meat, then refrigerate overnight, flipping at least once to help the flavors penetrate evenly.

3. Preheat the cooker to 225°F, low heat.

4. Remove the tri-tips from the marinade and discard the liquid. Fold the tri-tips into a C shape with any fat pointing out. Pierce the bottom and top of the tri-tips with the rotisserie rod, holding them in this shape, before securing with the rotisserie forks. Place the rotisserie rod on the cooker and place a water pan underneath. Cook until the tri-tip reaches an internal temperature of 145°F (USDA recommended) or your desired doneness. Medium-rare, which I prefer, is an internal temperature of 125°F.

5. Remove the meat from the cooker and let rest for about 20 minutes.

6. Raise the cooker's temperature to 400°F.

7. Returning the rotisserie rod to the heat source and sear each side of the tri-tips for 1 to 2 minutes to add a nice crust and some charring.

8. Slice the seared tri-tip against the grain into ¼- to ½-inch slices to serve.

SERVING TIP

Tri-tip has a very visible grain, which changes directions as it moves across the meat. When slicing your tri-tip, be mindful of the grain direction, so you can slice across the grain to get the most tender cut. You will need to change the direction of your slices as you cut.

PRIME RIB WITH HORSERADISH SAUCE

Serves: 8 to 10
Prep time: 20 minutes, plus 20 minutes to rest
Approximate cook time: 1 hour per pound
Cooker temperature: 225°F, low heat
Internal temperature: 145°F

For an incredible centerpiece for your next holiday meal, look no further than a juicy, tender, delicious prime rib roast. Prime rib is highly marbled and is a non-working muscle, meaning it is tender right from the start. Horseradish, accompanying beef since the 1600s, has a strong, spicy flavor that brings a sharp but pleasant contrast to the richness of the prime rib.

1 (8- to 10-pound) bone-in prime rib
1 cup Charcoal Beef Rub (page 107)
Olive oil (optional)
¼ cup plus 2 tablespoons sour cream
¼ cup mayonnaise
1 tablespoon prepared horseradish

1 tablespoon finely chopped fresh chives
2 teaspoons minced garlic
2 teaspoons grated lemon zest (from 1 lemon)
Juice of ½ lemon
Pinch kosher salt
Pinch cracked black pepper

1. Trim the thick fat cap on the top of the prime rib until it is about ¼ inch thick. If your prime rib hasn't come with the bones separated from the meat, slice between the bones and the meat about two-thirds of the way down the roast. This will make it easier to carve the meat later.

2. Preheat the cooker to 225°F, low heat.

3. Truss the prime rib tightly to fix the bones to the meat, with a tie between each bone (see Trussing, Roasts and Tenderloins, page 11). Liberally and evenly coat all sides of the full surface of the prime rib with the rub. If needed, use a thin layer of oil as a binder.

4. Pierce the prime rib through the center with a rotisserie rod and secure it with the rotisserie forks. Place the rotisserie rod on the cooker. Place a water pan underneath, so the cooker retains moisture.

5. While the beef cooks, in a small bowl, stir together the sour cream, mayonnaise, horseradish, chives, garlic, lemon zest, lemon juice, salt, and pepper. Store this, covered, in the refrigerator until ready to serve.

6. Cook until the prime rib reaches an internal temperature of 145°F (USDA recommended) or your desired doneness. Medium-rare, which I prefer, is an internal temperature of 125°F. Remove the prime rib from the heat, loosely tent with aluminum foil, and let rest for 20 minutes.

7. Raise the fire temperature to 400°F and return the prime rib to the cooker to sear the exterior for 1 to 2 minutes per side to build a crust.

8. To carve, snip the trussing and cut through the remaining one-third of the meat between the bones and the roast. Place the meat, cut-side down, on a cutting board before slicing off ½-inch slices, beginning on one end.

INGREDIENT TIP

Prime rib can get pricey, but right after a major holiday, like Christmas or Easter, its price is often heavily reduced. So, stock your freezer and save it for your next big event.

MARINATED STEAK SANDWICHES

Serves: 4 to 6
Prep time: 15 minutes, plus overnight to marinate
Approximate cook time: 10 minutes
Cooker temperature: 450°F, high heat
Internal temperature: 145°F

When I first moved to Australia, I lived in a tiny apartment in a run-down part of Queensland. There were very few places to eat within walking distance, but there was one spot that made incredible steak sandwiches. I ate their sandwiches so frequently that I started experimenting at home to create my own version. This recipe is my take on that steak sandwich, which, in my opinion, should, at minimum, always, always include quality steak, spicy mustard, and fresh arugula.

4 pounds skirt steak
2 tablespoons extra-virgin olive oil
2 tablespoons Worcestershire sauce
2 large garlic cloves, minced
1 tablespoon soy sauce
1 tablespoon balsamic vinegar

1 tablespoon paprika
1 tablespoon light brown sugar
2 teaspoons onion powder
2 teaspoons cracked black pepper
2 rosemary sprigs

OPTIONAL SANDWICH TOPPINGS

Caramelized onions
Caramelized peppers
Fresh arugula

Spicy English mustard
1 cup Basic Barbecue Sauce (page 104)
2 medium loaves sourdough bread, sliced

1. Trim any silver skin from the surface of the skirt steak and trim off any thick, firm pieces of fat.

2. In a large zip-top bag, combine the oil, Worcestershire, garlic, soy sauce, vinegar, paprika, brown sugar, onion powder, pepper, and rosemary to create a thick marinade. Add the skirt steak, seal the bag, removing all air from the bag, and massage the marinade into the steak. Refrigerate overnight, spreading out the steak inside the bag, so it marinates evenly.

3. Preheat the cooker to 450°F, high heat.

4. Remove the steak from the marinade and discard the liquid. Pierce the steak onto the rotisserie rod, focusing on keeping the rod in the center of the steak. Space it evenly (if it's in different pieces) to allow consistent cooking. Place the rotisserie rod on the cooker and cook until the steak reaches an internal temperature of 145°F (USDA recommended) or your desired doneness. Medium-rare, which I prefer, is an internal temperature of 125°F to 130°F. Don't be afraid to place the steak fairly close to the heat source at the end, as some char is a good thing.

5. Remove the steak from the cooker and let rest for 1 minute, before slicing it against the grain into ½-inch slices.

6. Layer some bread slices with any and all of your favorite sandwich toppings and finish with a nice layer of skirt steak.

SERVING TIP

Make your sandwiches infinitely better by toasting the bread before building the sandwiches. Liberally butter one side of the bread and place it in a hot cast-iron skillet until golden brown and crunchy.

GARLIC BUTTER-BASTED PRIME RIB AU JUS

Serves: 8 to 10
Prep time: 20 minutes, plus 20 minutes to rest
Approximate cook time: 1 hour per pound
Cooker temperature: 225°F, low heat
Internal temperature: 145°F

Prime rib and rib-eye steaks come from the same primal cut of beef. But unlike a steak, prime rib is cooked as a whole joint of meat, lacking the seared crust on both sides of a traditional steak. Still, a slow-roasted, reverse-seared prime rib is juicy and incredibly delicious. Au jus (meaning "with juice") is made with the drippings from the meat during cooking and is delicious when used as a gravy.

FOR THE PRIME RIB AND RUB

1 (8- to 10-pound) bone-in prime rib

2 cups (4 sticks) unsalted butter, at room temperature

7 garlic cloves, minced

2 heaping tablespoons ground mustard

1 tablespoon kosher salt

2 teaspoons cracked black pepper

2 rosemary sprigs, finely minced

2 thyme sprigs, finely minced

1½ cups beef stock

FOR THE AU JUS

¼ cup water

¼ cup no-sugar-added grape juice

1 tablespoon Worcestershire sauce

1. **To make the prime rib and rub:** Trim the thick fat cap on the top of the prime rib until it is about ¼ inch thick. If your prime rib hasn't come with the bone separated from the meat, slice between the bones and the meat about two-thirds of the way down the roast. This will make it easier to carve the meat later. Truss the prime rib tightly with a tie between each bone (see Trussing, Roasts and Tenderloins, page 11).

2. Preheat the cooker to 225°F, low heat.

3. In a medium bowl, stir together the butter, garlic, ground mustard, salt, pepper, rosemary, and thyme until a thick paste forms. Coat the full exterior of the prime rib with an even layer of the butter mixture. Pierce the prime rib through the center with the rotisserie rod and secure it with the rotisserie forks. Place the prime rib onto the cooker and place a water pan containing the stock underneath it.

4. Cook, basting the meat every 45 minutes to 1 hour with the drippings, until the prime rib reaches an internal temperature of 145°F (USDA recommended) or your desired doneness. Medium-rare, which I prefer, is an internal temperature of 125°F. Remove the prime rib from the heat, loosely tent with aluminum foil, and let rest for 20 minutes.

5. **To make the au jus:** While the meat rests, in a medium pot on a stovetop, combine the beef stock and drippings from the drip pan with the water, grape juice, and Worcestershire sauce. Bring to a simmer over medium heat, stirring constantly, and cook for 10 to 15 minutes, until the au just reduces by half.

6. Return the prime rib to the cooker, close to the heat source, and sear the exterior for 1 to 2 minutes per side to build a crust on all sides.

7. To carve, snip the trussing and cut through the remaining one-third of the meat between the bones and the roast. Place the roast, cut-side down, on the board and cut ½-inch slices, beginning on one end. Serve with the au jus.

SERVING TIP

This recipe is amazing as is but, if desired, slice the prime rib super thin and stack it onto a toasted bun. Dip the sandwich into the warm au jus for an amazing French dip.

CHAPTER 6

MARINADES, RUBS, AND SAUCES

GARLIC YOGURT SAUCE

Makes: 1 heaping cup (enough dip for about 6 people)
Prep time: 5 minutes, plus 1 hour to chill

Good barbecue comes from utilizing a variety of different ingredients and combining them to make a tasty and complex flavor profile. Use this simple sauce recipe to bring a zesty tart element to your dishes and cool down your palate when the spice gets you. Plus, this sauce makes a delicious dip with some carrot sticks and snap peas during the sometimes-lengthy wait for your meat.

1 cup plain Greek yogurt

2 tablespoons apple cider vinegar

2 heaping tablespoons dried mint leaves

1 teaspoon minced garlic

1 tablespoon sugar

In a medium bowl, stir together the yogurt, vinegar, mint, garlic, and sugar until well incorporated. Use the sauce immediately or refrigerate it, covered, for at least 1 hour, so the flavors can meld. Keep refrigerated in an airtight container for up to 2 days.

INGREDIENT TIP

Greek yogurt is best here because of its strong, tangy flavor. If Greek yogurt is hard to find, use regular plain yogurt and reduce the sugar by half.

SIMPLE BRINE

Makes: about 1 gallon
Prep time: 5 minutes
Cook time: 15 minutes, plus 2 hours to cool before use

One key to incredible low and slow barbecue is keeping the meat moist and juicy. This can be especially difficult for lean proteins such as pork and chicken, because the lack of internal marbling and fat allows the meat to dry out. To counter this dryness, brine the protein the night before cooking it. Brining allows the moisture inside the meat to bind with the absorbed salts, keeping the meat juicy and adding extra flavor.

10 cups water

8 cups apple juice

1½ cups kosher salt

½ cup packed light brown sugar

2 tablespoons black peppercorns

2 tablespoons mustard seeds

1. In a large stockpot, combine the water, apple juice, salt, brown sugar, peppercorns, and mustard seeds. Bring to a boil over high heat, reduce the heat to medium, and simmer for 5 minutes, until the salt and sugar dissolve.

2. Let the liquid cool fully, about 2 hours in the refrigerator, before adding the protein to it and refrigerating overnight. Discard the brine after each use.

PREPARATION TIP

Meat tends to float when placed in a liquid, so you may need to weigh it down to keep it submerged. The easiest way to do this is by topping the meat with a clean ceramic plate.

ALABAMA WHITE SAUCE

Makes: 2 cups (enough dipping sauce for about 12 people)
Prep time: 10 minutes
Cook time: 10 minutes, plus 30 minutes to cool

Unlike most barbecue sauces that have a tomato base, Alabama white sauce breaks the mold with its creamy mayonnaise base. Made famous by Big Bob Gibson Bar-B-Q in Decatur, Alabama, this now-ubiquitous sauce adds a zesty, sweet heat element to your barbecue and works especially well with chicken—but don't hesitate to experiment with it on other proteins and veggies.

1 cup mayonnaise

½ cup apple cider vinegar

¼ cup apple juice

1 tablespoon Dijon mustard

2 teaspoons prepared horseradish

1 teaspoon Worcestershire sauce

1 teaspoon cracked black pepper

½ teaspoon garlic powder

½ teaspoon hot sauce

½ teaspoon kosher salt

1. In a medium saucepan, stir together the mayonnaise, vinegar, apple juice, Dijon, horse-radish, Worcestershire sauce, pepper, garlic powder, hot sauce, and salt. Place the pan over medium heat and cook until the sauce reaches a simmer. Continue to simmer for 5 minutes, stirring constantly. Do not let the sauce boil.

2. Let the sauce cool to room temperature for about 30 minutes before using or storing.

3. Refrigerate in an airtight container for up to 5 days.

SERVING TIP

Before storing this sauce, let it cool to room temperature before putting it in the refrigerator. The sauce can become sour if refrigerated immediately.

ALL-PURPOSE RUB

Makes: ½ cup (enough for 1 medium chicken)
Prep time: 10 minutes

Barbecue separates itself from other cooking methods by cooking meat low and slow above an open flame. But what really takes barbecue to the next level is the extra layers of flavor brought to each dish using dry rubs, injections, and sauces. This simple rub brings together many of the traditional barbecue spices. And it's super versatile—you can add or remove ingredients to your heart's (or stomach's) content.

2 tablespoons kosher salt

1 tablespoon cracked black pepper

1 tablespoon garlic powder

1 tablespoon onion powder

1 tablespoon paprika

1 tablespoon ground mustard

1 tablespoon light brown sugar

2 teaspoons ground cumin

In a medium bowl, stir together the salt, pepper, garlic powder, onion powder, paprika, ground mustard, brown sugar, and cumin. Store the rub in an airtight container in a cool, dry place out of direct sunlight.

INGREDIENT TIP

Dry rub can last for 6 months or more, but you will notice, over time, that some of the ingredients begin to lose aroma and flavor.

BASIC BARBECUE SAUCE

Makes: 2½ cups (enough sauce for 15 people as a condiment)
Prep time: 10 minutes
Cook time: 10 minutes, plus 30 minutes to cool

Barbecue and sauce go together like Sonny and Cher, peanut butter and jelly, Batman and Robin, and hamburgers and fries. The combo is something far better than the sum of its parts. This simple barbecue sauce is sweet, tangy, easy to make, and so good you'll find yourself sneaking some with a spoon.

1 cup ketchup

¾ cup light brown sugar

⅓ cup molasses

3 tablespoons apple cider vinegar

1 tablespoon Worcestershire sauce

1 tablespoon ground mustard

2 teaspoons paprika

1 teaspoon minced garlic

1 teaspoon cracked black pepper

½ teaspoon kosher salt

Pinch ground cloves

1. In a medium saucepan, stir together the ketchup, brown sugar, molasses, vinegar, Worcestershire sauce, ground mustard, paprika, garlic, pepper, salt, and cloves. Place the pan over medium heat and cook until the sauce reaches a simmer. Continue to simmer for 5 minutes, stirring constantly. Do not let the sauce boil.

2. Let the sauce cool to room temperature for about 30 minutes before using or storing.

3. Refrigerate in an airtight container for up to 1 month.

SERVING TIP

Sure, barbecue sauce is great as dip or condiment, but don't hesitate to use this sauce as part of a marinade or (with a bit of corn syrup) as a simple rib glaze.

BLENDED CHIMICHURRI

Makes: 1½ cups (enough dipping sauce for 8 people)
Prep time: 15 minutes

This fresh condiment, attributed to Argentina and Uruguay, adds just that perfect flash of green herbs and zesty flavor to your red meat. Make this recipe in a food processor or with an immersion blender to keep the pieces small and let all the flavors mesh. It's delicious served with Picanha (page 81).

1 cup packed fresh parsley leaves

¼ cup packed fresh cilantro

4 garlic cloves, peeled

2 tablespoons chopped fresh oregano leaves

½ cup extra-virgin olive oil

3 tablespoons red wine vinegar

1 tablespoon red pepper flakes

Kosher salt

Cracked black pepper

1. In a blender or food processor, combine the parsley, cilantro, garlic, oregano, oil, and vinegar. Blend well. Add the red pepper flakes and season with salt and pepper to taste, then pulse briefly to combine

2. Refrigerate in an airtight container for up to 3 months. Before serving, whisk the sauce because it may separate.

SERVING TIP

Chimichurri is usually a dipping sauce for red meat, but it is great when mixed with mayonnaise for a creamy twist. Use your imagination: Add it to potatoes before roasting or drizzle it on pizza to liven it up.

BLACKBERRY GLAZE

Makes: 2 cups (enough glaze to coat 2 large rib racks)
Prep time: 10 minutes
Cook time: 10 minutes

Blackberries are one of my favorite fruits to use in barbecue. The sharp, sour flavor of the berry helps cut through the fattiness of the meat, while the sweetness amplifies the other savory flavors of the meat. Use this glaze as an alternative to the sauce in Carolina Chicken Wings (page 44), or replace the apricot preserves in the Mustard and Apricot Ham (page 66) for a delicious spin on the original recipe.

½ cup seedless blackberry preserves

½ cup ketchup

½ cup maple syrup

4 tablespoons (½ stick) unsalted butter

2 tablespoons apple cider vinegar

1 tablespoon Worcestershire sauce

1 tablespoon cracked black pepper

1 tablespoon hot sauce

1. In a blender or food processor, combine the blackberry preserves, ketchup, maple syrup, butter, vinegar, Worcestershire sauce, pepper, and hot sauce. Blend well.

2. Pour the sauce into a medium saucepan, place the pan over medium heat, and cook until the sauce comes to a simmer. Continue to simmer for 5 minutes, stirring constantly. Do not let the sauce boil. The glaze should be thick enough to cover the back of a spoon. As the glaze cools, it will thicken.

3. Refrigerate in an airtight container for up to 10 days.

PREPARATION TIP

Consistency of a finished glaze is key. If a glaze is too thick, it will not brush onto the meat easily. Too thin and it will run right off the meat. To thicken it, let it cook and reduce longer or add thickening agents like butter. To thin the glaze, stir in a little water or stock. Taste and adjust for seasoning as well.

CHARCOAL BEEF RUB

Makes: 1 cup (enough rub to coat 2 beef rib racks)
Prep time: 10 minutes

One of the best parts of barbecue is the bark that develops on the meat's exterior. This bark is dark and so can sometimes be mistaken for being burnt. Not so! Good barbecuers work hard to develop bark, but what they won't tell you is that adding one simple ingredient to your dry rub will almost guarantee a sumptuous bark: activated charcoal (see Ingredient Tip).

¼ cup kosher salt

¼ cup cracked black pepper

¼ cup ground cumin

¼ cup paprika

1 tablespoon plus 1 teaspoon garlic powder

1 tablespoon plus 1 teaspoon onion powder

1 tablespoon food-safe activated charcoal powder (optional)

2 teaspoons cayenne pepper

1. In a medium bowl, stir together the salt, black pepper, cumin, paprika, garlic powder, onion powder, charcoal powder (if using), and cayenne.

2. Store the rub in an airtight container in a cool, dry place out of direct sunlight.

INGREDIENT TIP

Look for a high quality, food-grade, finely ground charcoal powder. This dry rub can last for 6 months or more, but you will notice, over time, that some of the ingredients will begin to lose aroma and flavor.

MEASUREMENT CONVERSIONS

	US STANDARD	US STANDARD (OUNCES)	METRIC (APPROXIMATE)
VOLUME EQUIVALENTS (LIQUID)	2 TABLESPOONS	1 FL. OZ.	30 ML
	¼ CUP	2 FL. OZ.	60 ML
	½ CUP	4 FL. OZ.	120 ML
	1 CUP	8 FL. OZ.	240 ML
	1½ CUPS	12 FL. OZ.	355 ML
	2 CUPS OR 1 PINT	16 FL. OZ.	475 ML
	4 CUPS OR 1 QUART	32 FL. OZ.	1 L
	1 GALLON	128 FL. OZ.	4 L
VOLUME EQUIVALENTS (DRY)	⅛ TEASPOON		0.5 ML
	¼ TEASPOON		1 ML
	½ TEASPOON		2 ML
	¾ TEASPOON		4 ML
	1 TEASPOON		5 ML
	1 TABLESPOON		15 ML
	¼ CUP		59 ML
	⅓ CUP		79 ML
	½ CUP		118 ML
	⅔ CUP		156 ML
	¾ CUP		177 ML
	1 CUP		235 ML
	2 CUPS OR 1 PINT		475 ML
	3 CUPS		700 ML
	4 CUPS OR 1 QUART		1 L
	½ GALLON		2 L
	1 GALLON		4 L

OVEN TEMPERATURES

FAHRENHEIT	CELSIUS (APPROXIMATE)
250°F	120°C
300°F	150°C
325°F	165°C
350°F	180°C
375°F	190°C
400°F	200°C
425°F	220°C
450°F	230°C

WEIGHT EQUIVALENTS

U.S. STANDARD	METRIC (APPROXIMATE)
½ OUNCE	15 G
1 OUNCE	30 G
2 OUNCES	60 G
4 OUNCES	115 G
8 OUNCES	225 G
12 OUNCES	340 G
16 OUNCES OR 1 POUND	455 G

RESOURCES

HowLowCanYouSlow.com When I set out to write this book, I wanted to include everything needed to create incredible low and slow rotisserie barbecue dishes. Unfortunately, I found that it's not possible to encompass this in a book alone. To help with the techniques, recipe updates, equipment recommendations, and everything else you will need on your rotisserie journey, I have set up a website at HowLowCanYouSlow.com, which I update regularly. You can also see step-by-step video recipes and inspiration on my Instagram @_howlowcanyouslow, which includes some of the recipes in this book.

AmazingRibs.com Meathead and his team are incredible resources for understanding the science behind the art of low and slow barbecue.

MiguelsCookingWithFire.com Miguel Raya over at has an amazing style of cooking, crossing Mexican cuisine with low and slow smoked barbecue. Check out his website for a ton of delicious recipes.

OverTheFireCooking.com Derek Wolf takes cooking with fire to the next level, sharing a range of low and slow and hot and fast recipes. If you are ever in need of some recipe inspiration, check him out at

Binging with Babish has one of the most incredible YouTube channels, jam-packed with some of the most inspirational recipes you can imagine.

In the Mind of a Chef This series from Sean Brock provides some of the best insights into the values and community that comes from Southern cuisine and the history of fod in America.

A Meat Smoking Manifesto Aaron Franklin's book contains not only some amazing recipes, but also breaks down exactly what is going on inside your cooker and ways to get the most out of your barbecue.

INDEX

ACKNOWLEDGMENTS

I am so grateful for my amazing wife, Kylie, who stood by me and supported me as I wrote this book and tested the recipes. She has been a great sport, taste testing and giving advice. I truly couldn't have done it without her.

Special thanks to the Rockridge Press team for making this possible and for the invaluable support of their team of editors. This task would genuinely have been impossible without their support and guidance.

And a huge acknowledgement to the many low and slow barbecuers who have paved the way for people like me to be able to share my insights and recipes with you. Low and slow cooking is a long-lasting tradition that has brought so many communities together; I am grateful to be even just a small contributor to this legacy.

ABOUT THE AUTHOR

Jared Pullman is genuinely obsessed with low and slow smoked barbecue. When he's not in the middle of cooking something on his rotisserie, he's thinking about the next thing he can make and who he can share it with.

Born and raised in New Zealand, Jared now lives in Idaho with his incredible wife, Kylie, and their two dogs. Idaho may not be the most barbecue-orientated part of the United States, but you can usually find Jared doing his part to help change that.

If you have any questions about this book (or anything rotisserie-related), connect with Jared on Instagram @_howlowcanyouslow or at HowLowCanYouSlow.com.